Guilt

Guilt

Helping God's People Find Healing and Forgiveness

LEROY T. HOWE

Abingdon Press
Nashville

GUILT
HELPING GOD'S PEOPLE FIND HEALING AND FORGIVENESS

This book is printed on recycled, acid-free, elemental-chlorine-free paper.

Library of Congress Cataloging in Publication Data

Howe, Leroy T., 1936-
Guilt: helping God's people find healing and forgiveness / Leroy T. Howe.
p. cm.
ISBN 0-687-02594-X (pbk.: alk. paper)
1. Forgiveness—Religious aspects—Christianity. 2. Guilt—Religious aspects—Christianity. I. Title.

BV4647.F55H694 2003
253.5—dc21

2003011642

03 04 05 06 07 08 09 10 11 12—10 9 8 7 6 5 4 3 2 1

MANUFACTURED IN THE UNITED STATES OF AMERICA

In loving memory of Sarah Lynn Howe

Contents

FOREWORD

I began my seminary education when pastoral counseling was the new thing. My seminary was one of the earliest to have a full-time specialist in the field; we talked proudly in the dormitories that we were being taught not simply by someone with experience in pastoral care, but by someone who had a doctorate in the area. By the time I graduated from seminary, I was subscribing to two periodicals in pastoral psychology and belonged to a book club with monthly offerings in the same field.

But I was uneasy with what I had learned and with most of the published material that was coming my way. I didn't fault the professional competence of what I had learned or was reading, because I recognized that I wasn't knowledgeable enough to make such a judgment. But I was unhappy with the fact that there was so little substantial tie to biblical scholarship, and even less, it seemed to me, to Christian theology. I'm very sure that these shortcomings were not malicious. Those who were writing in the field were sometimes not equipped to venture too far into biblical or theological matters; besides, their enthusiasm for their new discipline made it easy for them to emphasize what was so exciting and (to use one of our contemporary terms) "on the cutting edge." And many of us pastors aided and abetted the problem because we were ourselves so caught up in what promised to be a vital new aid to our pastoral ministry.

As the years went by, I began (mercifully) to recognize my limits as a counselor. I came especially to realize that I was rarely giving my counselees the gifts I was most qualified to offer: compassion, understanding, faith, and prayer. I suspect it is significant that it was not a pastor who first raised significant questions about how we clergy were using this new field of learning, but a clinical psychologist at the prestigious Menninger Foundation, Paul Pruyser. He was concerned that so many pastors who came for specialized training were becoming "little psychiatrists," while neglecting their inherent strengths in theology and basic pastoral care.

Probably nowhere did some of us fail so badly as in our treatment of the experience of guilt. This failure is ironic because the biblical theologian is arguably more qualified than any other person to address the issues of guilt. It isn't that we invented guilt, though superficial critics sometimes say as much. No; the capacity for guilt is written into our genetic code, just as is our hunger to be better than we are. But we have a theology in both Judaism and Christianity that confesses the reality and importance of guilt, and how to deal with it constructively. When the psalmist cries, "Indeed, I was born guilty" (Ps. 51:5), you know that someone millennia ago understood the experience of guilt; and when that same writer pleads, "Restore to me the joy of your salvation" (Ps. 51:12), you realize that he or she also understood the place of healing.

But for a very long time, we pastoral counselors pulled back from even mentioning the word *guilt*. I suspect that some of us became equally cautious about confronting the subject in our preaching. In our neglect of the subject, we failed those persons whom we sought to counsel, and we left untended a field of knowledge in which we were potentially the most qualified to contribute.

This book by Leroy Howe goes a very long way toward remedying these faults and toward empowering the pastor or thoughtful layperson as counselor. Dr. Howe is a professional who knows how to bring together the fields of psychology and theology, and he does so in language that all of us can grasp. Better still, he addresses the issue of guilt realistically. In this, he is true to the Scriptures. The Bible is never a feel-good book, though some try to reduce it to that; it is a book that confronts life as we know it, sometimes with a toughness that offends our sensibilities. Dr. Howe is equally honest, kindly, mind you, but unflinching. He dares, for instance, to wrestle with the question of the "unpardonable sin" and reminds us that we never have the right to be unforgiving: "Withholding forgiveness is a divine prerogative exclusively."

Dr. Howe disposes of our modern or postmodern idea that if we just come to know enough, we will do what is right. "Too often," he writes, "we use our reasoning powers not to determine the most honorable actions, but to rationalize our dishonorable ones." I recognize the truth of this saying because I have so often seen people who were guilty of such rationalizing; but worse, because I have myself been guilty. I know it's a good book when it reads me so accurately.

But most of all, Dr. Howe sets us on a right course regarding guilt. He uses a marvelous term: *"our God-given capacity to feel guilt."* Guilt is not our enemy, not if we recognize it for what it is and learn how to profit from its ministry to us. Guilt is that voice that pleads with us to face ourselves honestly, then to make right whatever wrongs we have done to others. A proper response to feelings of guilt can help us along the way to true personality growth and to admirable maturity. Indeed, such a response will open the door to those most elusive qualities of righteousness and true holiness.

I heard enough revival preaching in my youth to know something about guilt, both real and induced. As a pastor, I have counseled with people who were struggling with guilt they had no reason to feel. Far more often, I have counseled with people who needed to feel guilt so they would deal honorably with their conduct. This book takes on both kinds of problems. As such, it will benefit the pastoral or lay counselor both as a counselor and as an individual seeking to be a better Christian.

The closing chapter deals with a painful subject—those instances in which the church is the wrongdoer. Few things are more painful to a perceptive pastor than the realization that the church, which ought to be a hospital for the wounded, is sometimes the source of wounding. In my more recent years as a seminary professor, I have discovered that a theological seminary can be guilty of this same sin. I suspect this is also true of any confessedly Christian college or Christian retirement community. Our Christian institutions are not exempt from hurting the persons we're supposed to serve; and when we do hurt them, the hurt is likely to be the deepest and most grievous of all simply because we're supposed to be a refuge, not a battleground.

So I'm grateful for this book. It is honest, it is theologically sound, it is pastorally compassionate, and it is intellectually accessible. I wish it had been available when I graduated from seminary.

J. Ellsworth Kalas

Preface

Tad and Beth are sitting in their pastor's office, tired, but reluctant to take a break in the conversation. With the pastor's help, they have been making progress over the past few months, working through grief over the death of their son in an accident caused by an intoxicated driver. Now, their primary issue is changing, from grief to guilt.

Haltingly, Tad and Beth confess how guilt-stricken they are over their bitterness toward the driver, their contempt for a system that allows people with DUI convictions to drive at all, and their inability to find any sign of forgiveness in their hearts. It is his judgmentalism that is so disturbing for Tad: *I know they had to put this guy away for what he's done, but aren't we still supposed to forgive him because he is a human being, a child of God? I can't do it, Pastor, I just can't do it! I really thought I was a better Christian than this.*

Beth chides Tad for being so hard on himself, and especially for not seeing that forgiveness in this situation would be only cheap grace: *He's a really, truly, terribly guilty man, and he has to face the consequences of what he's done. Forgiveness is what the system keeps doling out, and it hasn't helped anybody; all it does is deny the seriousness of what problem drinkers do*. And yet, like Tad, Beth is also appalled over how hateful she feels toward her son's killer: *But Jesus came to forgive people, didn't he? It's all about grace, isn't it? How can I keep showing up at church as grace-less as I am?*

It heightens this couple's pain that the man who caused their son's death denies any responsibility for his actions: *The kid should have known I was coming through the intersection. He had plenty of time to stop. I'm sorry about what happened, but it wasn't my fault! It was his!* After a jury disagreed with this rationalization, and a judge assigned a severe punishment to the offender, the prosecutor sought to reassure Tad and Beth by telling them, *You can take comfort in the fact that justice has been done*. That they cannot take such comfort only makes them feel worse. Tad and Beth believe strongly that they must forgive the man who brought so much hurt into their lives, even though the man shows no signs of remorse. They are overwhelmed with guilt for not being able to take even a first step.

What could any of us say to this anguished couple, and to caring people like them who are struggling to forgive others' devastating carelessness? What do we say when the cause of their suffering is not just carelessness, but malevolence, for example, to a woman burdened by guilt for not forgiving the hopped-up teenager who clubbed her parents to death in a botched robbery? To a man who believes he is going to hell for not forgiving the priest who abused him as a child? This book is about helping people offer and accept forgiveness without undervaluing the significance of harmful actions, our accountability for them, and the importance of preventing their recurrence. It is also about helping guilty people come to terms with their guilt, while never losing sight of their worthiness in the sight of God.

The latter concern is particularly poignant when the guilty parties are members and leaders of our own congregations. Tad and Beth's pastor must grapple with just this issue, for the driver who killed their son is chairperson of their church's Parish Council. The work ahead for this pastor is daunting. He must continue to minister effectively to this still grieving, guilt-ridden couple. At the same time, he must find a way to help his errant parish leader become a more responsible human being. Finally, he must provide his congregation with the leadership necessary for its members to work out an authentically Christian response to the guilty member in their midst. Thus, this book is not only about helping victimized people become more forgiving, and helping guilty people become more accountable. It is also about helping Christian congregations express their collective forgiveness with due regard for the responsibility of their members to conduct themselves "in a manner worthy of the gospel of Christ" (Phil. 1:27).

Chapter 1 explores how and why, in spite of our avoiding, denying, and projecting them, guilt feelings play an essential role in the process of developing a healthier inner self and of achieving reconciliation in relationships broken by wrongdoing. Chapter 2, in showing the relationship between wrongdoing, guilt, and free will perversely misused, discusses how God's gift of freedom is both a glorious and a mixed blessing.

Chapter 3 characterizes the normal steps that lead wrongdoers and those whom they wrong toward reconciliation and brings into focus situations beyond which these steps cannot take us. Chapter 4 contrasts the process of reconciliation with two widely used, unhelpful strategies for dealing with guilt: assuming too little of it and assuming too much of it.

Chapters 5 and 6 discuss in detail the fundamental affirmation of this book, that guilt is better healed by forgiveness than it is by demanding and by making amends. From this discussion, chapter 7 derives practical strategies for helping people whose guilt, guilt feelings, and unresolved anger impede their personal growth and jeopardize their relationships.

The final chapter of the book is about pastoral leadership in congregations and church institutions burdened by the offenses of their own members and leaders. It attempts to deal forthrightly with some of the most difficult issues that pastors must face every day: calling their parishioners to accountability in their own lives; challenging their parishioners to oppose, with them, the sins of the institutional church whenever and wherever such sins occur; and helping people who have been wronged by the church to forgive the wrongs done to them.

Guilt: Helping God's People Find Healing and Forgiveness can be read for personal enrichment and spiritual growth by both pastors and laypersons; it can serve as the basis for study courses; and it can be used in conjunction with pastors' training and supervision of lay caregivers in their congregations. For this latter purpose, the material complements my earlier book on lay shepherding, *A Pastor in Every Pew: Equipping Laity for Pastoral Care*.

ACKNOWLEDGMENTS

Two groups of faithful Christians have inspired this book. In the first are students too numerous to name individually, with whom I had the privilege of working during almost thirty years as a faculty member of the Perkins School of Theology at Southern Methodist University. I hope that the chapters to follow do at least partial justice to the integrity of their own ministries of forgiveness and reconciliation in the church today.

The second group is composed of the lay caregivers of First United Methodist Church, Richardson, Texas, along with the church's Senior Pastor, Dr. Clayton Oliphint. Several members of this much-cherished fellowship—Earnest Deadwyler, Walter Evans, Chris Guldi, Bonnie Hegler, and the Reverend Debra Hobbs Mason—provided invaluable suggestions for making the book helpful to lay caregivers as well as to pastors. Jean Macy and Robert Macy kept me on track through the subsequent drafts of the manuscript. My wife, Nancy Howe, edited the final version with the patience, compassion, good humor, faith, and understanding that continue to make our home a haven of blessing and peace.

CHAPTER ONE

THE DEVICES AND DESIRES OF OUR OWN HEARTS

Of all God's gifts to us, the one for which we are only rarely thankful is the capacity to feel guilt. It is easy to understand this lack of gratitude. Guilt feelings are distressing to endure because they remind us of two particularly painful facts about ourselves. One is that we do things that bring harm to ourselves and others and jeopardize relationships in the process. The other is that we are not yet the kind of men and women that we can be and should be, that our Creator means us to be. Some people give such scrupulous attention to these facts that they are difficult to be around for very long. Other people pay so little attention to these same facts that they are dangerous to be around at all. The purpose of this first chapter is to show why our vulnerability to guilt feelings, for all the discomfort it can bring us, is nevertheless something for which to be profoundly grateful.

Astray Like Lost Sheep

Traditionally, to express the truth about the human condition—that we are not what we are created to be—Christians have used familiar confessional language such as: "Almighty and most merciful Father, we have erred and strayed from thy ways like lost sheep." Today, many people are put off by language like this. Less disconcerting to them are the kinds of things I hear frequently from students, friends, counselees, and coworkers in ministry, such as:

> *I want to be, and can be, so much more than I am right now.*
>
> *It's tough struggling not to fall back into all those old ways of doing things that gave me so many problems. But I'm working at it and making pretty good progress.*
>
> *I used to beat myself up a lot for not making more of my life, but, you know, I finally decided just to slow down, take things one step at a time, and accept small victories instead of demanding huge successes all at once.*

At first glance, statements like these suggest insight and accountability. But there are several things lacking in them. First, instead of drawing our attention to the universal condition of fallibility, failure, and malfeasance, which all of us share as human beings, the statements emphasize individual resolution simply to do better from here on and not worry about past mistakes, misdoings, and mistreatment. Second, they show little awareness of how serious the flaws in us are that they naively envision overcoming. Instead, they significantly overvalue what moral resoluteness can accomplish all on its own. The real truth about ourselves is more sobering and more painful. It is that, in spite of all our best intentions, we persistently and consistently fall short of

- fulfilling others' expectations of us;
- fulfilling our own expectations of ourselves;
- doing all that is necessary in order to realize worthy personal goals;
- living up to our own highest ideals and principles;
- meeting our legitimate responsibilities to family members, friends, and all who have need of us; and
- honoring God in the ways that God deserves to be honored.

Restricting our confession of faults only to sporadic and forgettable incidents of falling short, pledging earnestly to work harder on becoming a better person, and expecting others to judge us by our sincerity, rather than by our effectiveness, only trivializes the difference between what we think we can make of ourselves and what God is striving to make of us.

Finally, what is missing in the statements above is a clear sense of discomfort, distress, and even despair about the scope and magnitude of what we need to change about ourselves. At best, these statements contain only the barest hint that our wrongdoing to ourselves and others can be "grievous unto us." The fact is, however, that we are not *mere* offenders against our best interests and those of others. We are *miserable* offenders who are called to be "heartily sorrowful" for our misdoings. The self-congratulatory statements cited above minimize the darkness of our condition as human beings and the difficulties awaiting us on the road to restoration, through Christ, to our true nature as bearers of God's own image.

Crucial, then, for our personal growth and our relationship with God is our willingness to be and feel "convicted" of our manifold wrongdoing. In a bygone era, communities of faith raised up many wise, compassionate, and truthful witnesses to help us deal with the many unpleasant realities about ourselves. Sadly, reliable companions and guides for this journey are relatively scarce today.

On the one hand, there are multitudes of caregivers in both the mental health professions and our churches who—for the most part, unintentionally—distract us with countless soothing assurances that are even more inhibiting to our spiritual development than the kinds of statements previously quoted. Rather than offering us pallid, but relatively innocuous, translations of traditional confessional language, these assurances go much further. They seem to be bent on either covering over or denying outright the fact that we have fallen far short of being the men and women God wants us to be, for example:

> *We're not bad people, you know, even though sometimes we do things that we regret. Concentrate on what you can become now, and forget about the kind of person you were before.*
>
> *You can't change the mistakes you've already made, but you can learn from them and move on. Cut out all this blaming of yourself, OK?*
>
> *"Guilting" people is never a good idea, least of all giving yourself a case of the "guilties."*

Precisely because there is some truth, and important truth at that, in each of these statements, it is easy to become convinced that they capture the whole truth about human beings. To those so convinced, it is only the spiritual spoilsports among us who keep harping on the seamier sides of human behavior. Once, a cherished friend expressed this point of view to me in a strikingly succinct and winsome way: *I think guilt and blame are going the way of the dodo bird, and we're finally living in a time when we can just celebrate our goodness and learn to appreciate everybody, no matter what.*

On the other hand, just as there are caring people who treat the bleakness of human wrongdoing as if either it does not exist at all or it does not matter very much, there are others who focus only on the worst in human nature. They criticize and blame others mercilessly, feeding like predators on others' faults and only rarely admitting any of their own. These are the highly judgmental, pharisaical keepers of God's ledger sheets against all the rest of us, whose self-appointed mission in life seems to be that of drawing our attention to just how extensive our wrongdoing is. Around people like this for very long, even the most self-confident can become bewitched by notions of how worthless we all are in God's sight and how hopeless our future is, short of miracles for which we are too despicable to ask and which we are too despairing to anticipate.

Certainly, it is misleading to accentuate only our positive features at the expense of acknowledging our shortcomings. But, as the following example shows, it can be downright crippling to dwell on our failings so much that our vision of God's liberating plan for us becomes blurred beyond recognition and celebration. Sophie grew up in the stifling religious atmosphere of a church community fanatically preoccupied with finding and rooting out sin everywhere. After years of spiritual struggle, hardship, and desolation, she finally found a healthy parish to welcome, support, and challenge her. One time, in the course of telling me more about her very troubled life, Sophie said some things that I still find both extraordinarily insightful and moving, as well as disturbing:

> *There have to be a lot of people out there like me, who were taught to believe that we're all just hanging in the air on an unraveling rope until God makes up his mind whether to give us any breaks at all, or just gives up on us because we're so rotten and sends us all to hell. And you know what the worst of that outlook is? It's the fact that the people who promote it are always in the clear. They're the perfect ones and all the*

rest of us are wicked and damned. It's taken me a long time to begin to see things more clearly.

Even in today's era of positive thinking, feeling good, and taking care of ourselves first, many people live their lives bombarded by negatives, either from others, themselves, or both. Rather than feel the occasional discomfort, distress, or even despair that signals their having done something that they ought not to have done or their failing to do something that they ought to have done, they suffer constant reminders of their mistakes, weaknesses, corruption, and utter impotence to change for the better. To these suffering souls, constant fretting about not doing the right thing substitutes for living gratefully and graciously, as their faith collapses into appeasing a frustrated, disappointed, angry God. In order to ease the pain of their self-criticism, some people become more judgmental toward others than they are toward themselves, and the cycle of blaming and shaming continues.

Feeling Guilty When We Should Feel Guilty

Even though the Christian message is primarily about release from bondage to our sins, it also emphasizes the positive role that a sense of guilt about them plays in our relationship with the One who redeems us from them. As we have seen, many people do not find this emphasis to their liking. Instead of cultivating a healthy gratitude for the new light that Jesus Christ sheds on guilt—that God spares those who confess their faults—they direct their spiritual energies toward insulating themselves from guilt feelings altogether. For them, offensive and harmful acts are mere mistakes, reflecting only momentary lapses of temper. What counts is sincerity, not how individual actions turn out, for example:

> *Things just didn't happen like I thought they would. What else can I say?*
>
> *Yes, I did some things that I wish I hadn't, but I never intended anybody any harm.*
>
> *Hey, we all make mistakes. Don't take what I did so seriously.*

One of my most fondly remembered theological colleagues, Albert Outler, once referred to people who talk like this as members of a new, guiltless generation, for whom trying to do better in the future makes repentance, confession, and penance both unnecessary and unseemly in the present.

To be sure, exclamations of guiltlessness like those just quoted are appropriate in response to unfair criticism or to someone's attempt to shift blame away from himself or herself to us. They can be especially helpful in warding off religious sadists whose greatest pleasure seems to come from driving people to their knees in self-abnegation. As a troubled parishioner, Chris, expressed it to his pastor, Jill, one afternoon:

> *You can't believe what it was like growing up in that church. Little things, big things, unimportant things, important things—it didn't matter. We never got any of them right. Eventually I got the hang of shrugging it all off and saying some dumb thing like, "C'mon, I'm only human, you know. Give me a break." Then, I really got smart and took some courses at the seminary. Know what I learned there? That all is forgiven, except maybe berating ourselves, and that we're free from bondage to the Law and everything else. The relief was overwhelming.*

Or at first it was, anyway. But now? What brought Chris to talk with Jill was his fear that, by throwing off the shackles of excessive guilt feelings, he might no longer be able to feel guilt at all. *Deciding not to dwell unhealthily on our faults is one thing*, he said, *but refusing to hold ourselves responsible at all for what we do is quite another.*

Chris's "guilt switch" is working just as it should. The alarm it set off inside him directed his attention to the real danger of minimizing guilt: losing that sense of accountability to others that strengthens respect for their fundamental dignity and rights and of our obligation to defend them. Turning away from facing our guilt when we do wrong to people makes us increasingly vulnerable to using them for self-centered purposes. Dismissing our transgressions against others from our mind, we focus instead on others' transgressions against us and devote our energies to rendering them impotent to transgress further. Getting them before they get us becomes the rule. *I know people like this right now,* Chris lamented, *and I'm afraid I'm becoming one of them.* The conversation continued:

> *Jill: Say a little more about the kind of folks we're talking about here.*
> *Chris: The kind that puts down talk about God's mercy and kindness.*
> *J: In what way?*
> *C: By saying that it's only for the weak-willed and the bleeding hearts.*
> *J: Kind of like, never concede and never explain.*
> *C: Yeah, only losers do that.*
> *J: No wonder you've been upset. A guy who believes this kind of stuff isn't the kind of guy you want to be.*
> *C: I guess I've been losing sight of the fact that God's forgiveness has to go on constantly, that it's not a once and for all thing. And that means that however liberated I think we are, I'm still doing things that I need to ask forgiveness for.*
> *J: Guilt feelings aren't so bad after all?*
> *C: Thank God.*

If we are to experience fully the abundant life that God has promised us in Jesus Christ, then we must be willing to overcome our obliviousness to, denial of, and self-righteousness about pursuing our own causes at others' expense. We must keep the remembrance of our wrongdoing before us, acknowledge honestly the guilt that our wrongdoing evokes, and bear with heavy hearts accountability for injecting our wrongfulness into a world that would be much the better without it. All of this should remind us that spiritual abundance is the fruit of diligent and arduous effort as well as of God's ever-present grace and love. Its principal nutrient is self-knowledge, often acquired at considerable pain. As a preacher of old reminds us, "in much wisdom is much grief: and he that increaseth knowledge increaseth sorrow" (Eccles. 1:18 KJV).

We Shall Know the Truth, Whether We Want to or Not

Can we make ourselves vulnerable enough to confront the most grievous truth of all about human existence in the world—that by our wrongdoing we continue to deface the divine image in us—and not be overwhelmed in the process? Faith's answer to this question is that we have always had within us, and continue to have, the resources we need for the task. For God is constantly renewing in our inner being the capacity to seek and confront the full truth about ourselves, however disconcerting, humbling, and even traumatizing some of that truth may be, when it is fully laid bare before us. We truly are wrongdoers in God's eyes. God truly does hold us responsible for everything we leave undone that we should do and for everything we do that we should not do. And—most important—God has created us with the capacity both to know these painful truths about ourselves and to respond to them in the way that he desires of us.

Creating humanity in God's own image and likeness, God endows every human being with the desire to know the truth. Even when the truths that we must confront are distressing, the desire to know them still surges in us. For philosophers through the ages, this is the one desire among all others that defines our humanness. For the Yahwist in Genesis, the desire to know is the primary source of the first couple's questioning their creator about the fruits of knowledge. It is the origin of our every urge to "taste and see" for ourselves how things are. It is the spur to restless skepticism in the face of every ill-conceived notion, idea, precept, rule, law, doctrine, or worldview that any self-absorbed, power-abusing ideologue or demagogue has ever attempted to impose arbitrarily upon us.

Equipping us with a strong desire to know the truth, God also encourages us to seek truth on our own, calls us to celebrate it wherever we find it, and cajols us to shape our lives in accord with it, at whatever personal sacrifices we must make to let truth make us free. From the seeking, the celebrating, and the shaping comes some of the most precious fruit of all, the fruit of understanding and wisdom. Given that we are not only fallible creatures, but finite ones as well, we can never achieve the infinite knowledge that enriches the life of God—although we lust after such and sometimes delude ourselves into thinking that we already possess it. We do, however, possess genuine and lasting knowledge of many things. Some of it we acquire on our own, and some of it we receive from God.

Among the many kinds of things that we do know, one of the most important is, in the words of an ancient prophet, what the Lord "requires" of us (Mic. 6:8). In making covenant with a people God chose to be his special representatives in the world, the Old Testament tells us, God revealed decisively how we should strive to live, not as innocents in a Paradise free from all dangers, conflict, and toil, but as participants in an inherently ambiguous historical process fraught with challenges and threats, encompassing nothing less than the whole of humankind on earth. That we do not live up to all of God's expectations does not alter the fact that we know what those expectations are. That we may become confused by what others teach us about God's law does not alter the fact that God sets that law deep within us, writing it on our very hearts (Jer. 31:33). For Paul, God does this from the very beginning (Rom. 1:20-21).

Why Knowing the Truth Is Not Always Enough

When the issue is what we must do in order to honor and please our Creator, we cannot evade our responsibility by pleading ignorance. In Paul's words, we are "without excuse." Nevertheless, we make excuses all the time for doing what we know we should not do and for failing to do what we know we should; for example, we weren't born smart enough, we didn't get taught the right things, we ran with the wrong crowd, we started bad habits that we can't overcome, we never had an even break, nobody ever really cared about us, and on and on. Too often, we use our reasoning powers not to determine the most honorable actions, but to rationalize our dishonorable ones.

If all human beings are created with the capacity to seek and find truth in general, and to respond to the revelation of the specific truths that God deems essential to a relationship with him, how can we misuse our rational powers so egregiously? How can so many of us so much of the time be so confused about who and whose we are and what our exalted place in creation requires of us? How can so many basic questions about human relationships and destiny provoke perpetual and tedious disagreements, generate conflicts and wars, and still remain unanswered in spite of the best efforts of the most thoughtful, honest, and conscientious among us?

These are important questions, so important that leaving them unanswered has serious spiritual consequences. If we can offer no explanation for people persistently acting as if they do not know better, when in fact they do know better, we can all too easily dismiss our own wrongfulness as just one more of life's unfortunate mysteries that no one can do anything about. The fact of the matter, however, is that we do know why we commit acts for which we must rationalize. We do know why we become lost in our own rationalizations. We do know why we deform disagreements about what truth is for particular situations into the altogether false conclusion that there is no normative truth at all.

The basic answer to the question of why we offer up excuses for our wrongdoing, when we are in fact without excuse, is this: Our God-given freedom includes the power not to use it as God intends it to be used. Just as we are fully capable of knowing ourselves as God knows us, and to know and do what God requires of us, we are also fully free not to exercise the capacity, not to honor the truths discovered by means of it, and not to act on the basis of either our best knowledge or any knowledge at all. In essence, we are created with the power both to do and not to do what we know we should do. Two corollaries of this affirmation speak directly to our substituting rationalization for obedience to God. The first is that habitual misuse of our power to know and to do what God requires of us eventually contaminates the entire process of discovering, holding onto, and honoring truth. The second is that reversing the process requires not so much an increase of intellectual effort as it does a deep and abiding respect for the feeling of guilt.

The ancient philosopher Plato once conjured an intriguing idea about the relationship between knowledge and soul formation. He posited that our souls gradually conform to the kinds of objects that our minds habitually contemplate. For example, Plato believed, if we continuously direct our thoughts to the things of the physical world, our souls will become too materialistic in outlook to respond to higher, spiritual realities. At the end of this insidious process, we forget the spiritual realm at all and become slaves to impulses rather than servants of principles.

We do not have to agree with all of Plato's theories about human knowing in order to glean from them one particularly important insight, that restricting our relationships to the most mundane aspects of earthly existence can have a profoundly corrupting effect on our capacity to understand and take delight in what transcends the finite, the transient, and the corruptible. To put this insight in Christian terms, we do not take our bearings from the knowledge that God intends us to possess because, like Demas, we set our hearts too much on this present world (2 Tim. 4:10). Or, like still others that Paul had in mind in this same letter, we stop our ears from hearing truth, turn instead to fables, and follow our own whims (4:3-4).

Plato believed that the solution to the problem of a weakened and corrupted mind is always more and better thinking. For him, only our rational side can transform our irrational one. Ancient Israel and the Christian tradition know better. Minds weakened by wrongdoing are strengthened only by reversing the wrongdoing itself, a process that requires the mobilization not so much of intellect, but of will and, more specific, of a will bent on overcoming feelings of guilt by right action. Regret, remorse, owning up, making amends, and experiencing forgiveness restore our mental faculties to their proper functioning more effectively than rationally derived insight ever can.

Guilt feelings contain enormous power both for good and for ill in our lives. By assaulting us constantly with searing reminders of how alienated we are from God, they can drive us to despair over ever fulfilling God's hopes for us. But they can also help us break through the excuses, rationalizations, and self-delusions we use to avoid coming to terms with our higher nature. They can force us to take seriously our calling to live in the image of Jesus Christ's perfect humanness and to become more effective caregivers to people whose guilt and guilt feelings cry out for both attention and resolution.

Summary

Just as we are like our Creator in the capacity to enjoy knowledge, we are also like him in the capacity to exercise freedom of choice and action. It is in the realm of deciding, taking action, and assuming responsibility for the consequences of our actions that our God-given capacity to feel and acknowledge guilt makes its most important contribution to our spiritual growth. In specific, our capacity to feel guilt is God's principal means of ensuring that we will not misuse his great gift of freedom to fashion lives that only dimly approximate the glorious life offered us in Christ. We have the power not to do and not to be what God desires, but we do not have the power to be disobedient to God without feeling guilt about it. Just what it means to bear the image of God as creatures endowed with freedom at all, and why God risked endowing us with it in the first place, is the primary subject of the next chapter.

CHAPTER TWO

FREEDOM MISUSED, PEOPLE ABUSED

Guilt feelings are a sign of wrongs that need righting and a means of motivating wrongdoers to right them. As this chapter explores, they are also a sign of freedom and responsibility. We are responsible for our actions because we have been created with the freedom to act on the basis of choice and not only from instinct, caprice, and compulsion. When we misuse our freedom and act irresponsibly, therefore, it is in our very nature to feel guilt.

That we are free means that we have within us the power to love God wholly, to love ourselves and our neighbors as God loves us, to seek his will for all of creation diligently and with grateful hearts, to obey him joyfully, to pursue justice for all with every resource of mind and will, and to dwell humbly in the world God has given us. It also means, though, that we have within us the power to value our own choices over God's will, to pursue our own interests instead of seeking God's plan for us, to insist on a future of our own making rather than to cherish the future that God's only son has opened to us, to hate rather than to love, and to revere evil more than good.

When we stare into the horrors that the evilly inclined can and do inflict everywhere in the world, we may wonder whether freedom is really worth the cost to those who suffer others' misuse of it. Granted that human freedom is truly a glorious gift, we might ask, how can the One who bestows it be deserving of homage when he seems so unwilling or unable or both to protect those who use their freedom wisely from those who do not? This chapter seeks to bring the resources of our faith to dealing with this issue, for the purpose of showing that the healing of guilt must include recovery of the power to use freedom wisely.

Is Freedom Really Worth the Risk?

It is easy to understand why, face-to-face with tragedies instigated by willfully destructive people, we can become angry with God for not preventing people from doing harm to one another. We can easily fantasize about being wholly protected recipients of a world with no pain, no worry, and no risk, but with freedom to pursue opportunities, enjoy challenges, and decide things on our own. The problem is that we cannot have genuine freedom and at the same time be fully protected from its misuse. The very meaning of freedom includes the power to use it for ill as well as for good. Unless we can choose both, we are free to do neither.

For many people, the way that true freedom works is profoundly unsettling. It presents too many uncertainties. More comforting, perhaps, is the vision of a God who is so utterly in control of everything that, for instance, not a single sparrow falls to the ground by accident and not a single hair on our heads goes unnumbered (Matt. 10:29-30). According to this vision of God's absolute sovereignty, everything happens for a reason, even the destructive consequences of people's misuse of their freedom.

With sufficient faith, we can always see how the wrong "that seems oft so strong" serves only higher, positive purposes.

From the sixteenth century to the present, mainstream Protestantism has defended one or more articulations of this vision with great vigor. Common to most of the defenses is the view that unless God is behind everything that happens anywhere and at anytime, chaos alone will rule. Freedom and indeterminacy contradict faith's foundational conviction that God is sovereign over all and needs nothing from us in order for his purposes to be achieved. The problem with this staggeringly problematic interpretation of divine providence—one that leaves human freedom out of the picture altogether—is that the alternative it so disparages is actually more credible than it itself is.

Christians who work hard enough at it may be able to convince themselves, at least for a while, that believing in God's absolute rule is the most powerful bulwark available to us against the anxiety, anger, and despair that human malevolence elicits in its victims. Furthermore, they may be able to offer at least some solace to others in need of assurance about God's presence in our lives, for example:

> *God will take care of everything. You'll see. All we have to do is trust him, and things will work out all right.*
>
> *How can finite minds like ours grasp the whole picture like God does? We just have to believe that he is present in all things and that he always knows what he's doing, and we should be grateful that we're a part of it all.*
>
> *Someday God's going to explain it all to us, and then we'll understand why.*

In countless situations, statements like these provide much needed comfort. But the comfort they offer can only be fleeting at best because sooner or later we have to deal with a thoroughly repugnant implication contained in each of them. If everything that happens, happens for a divine purpose, then God's plan for humanity somehow includes lying, cheating, stealing, neglecting, abusing, raping, torturing, murdering, and terrorizing, since these things have been going on for a very long time.

In the long run, it cannot be comforting to thoughtful people to contemplate that everything is an expression of an almighty and benevolent will beyond human understanding. Are we seriously to believe, for example, that God has some good reason in mind for raising up prophets to proclaim "death to infidels" and for withholding the reason from the rest of us? By way of more modest illustrations:

> *Bill lives alone in a dingy apartment complex littered with the detritus of an inner city plagued with unrelieved poverty, out-of-control gangs, family violence, omnipresent drugs, indifferent law enforcement, and rapidly escalating hopelessness. His surroundings, however, do not seem to bother him much. For thirty years, Bill has wandered aimlessly, struggling to accept his becoming an object of repugnance for fighting in a war that he, his friends, and his family members opposed and that his leaders despaired of ever winning.* I didn't start it. Nobody wanted to be in it. Our country had no business going there. But somehow, it's my fault, Bill reiterates. I'm supposed to believe that God put us there?

> *Darlene leaves yet another meeting of Mothers Against Drunk Driving with no peace in her soul. It is now ten months since her only child was run down in the street by a car whose intoxicated driver, with no apparent hesitation and with three previous DUI convictions behind him, left the scene before the police and ambulance arrived. Two of her closest friends, strong Christians, still have not been able to comfort her in the name of Christ. It is little wonder. Most typically, their words to Darlene are:* Our God is so powerful and loving, Darlene. Just think, he's guided that driver to commit his life for Christ. Who would have thought that anything

> like that would even be possible? Billy didn't die in vain. It just has to be part of God's plan for all of us.
>
> *Henry is still waking up several times at night, perspiring and trembling, with flashbacks to the tower from which he escaped only moments before it collapsed. Over a hundred of his office colleagues, many of them close personal friends, died in the conflagration. Henry resists talking about the incident in the way that his pastor does:* How long will we continue to reject the truth that God is plainly revealing to us? We are in the last days, the long prophesied end of history as we know it. Our God is a great God who has inflicted this terrible evil to awaken mankind everywhere to what is yet to come.

Might it not be better, instead of believing in the God whom the statements above seek to glorify, to believe in no God at all? For many thoughtful people, the only credible answer to the question just posed is an unqualified *yes!* As a beloved colleague in the university that we inhabited together for many years once put it:

> *I really do want to believe that what you call the* "God of the theologians" *may not be the* God *who truly is, but I've never been able to get to that big* God *except through just what these little theologians say about him, that he's the one who's in charge of everything. Well, if this is what it means to be in charge—causing all the evil things that evil people do in the world—then I have to say no thanks, and I'll take my chances with randomness and chaos.*

There is available to us a more adequate and uplifting way of thinking about human existence in the world than either celebrating God as the One who controls everything or resigning ourselves to the conclusion that "things just happen—so what?" or bemoaning God's noninterventions in situations screaming for his direct action. The better way than any of these is the way of praising God for making us free agents in the world and not mere passive recipients of an absolute determination of everything that goes on in it. It is the way of seeing, accepting, and celebrating the divine valuing of human freedom in the midst of our every struggle with the consequences of its misuse. The fuller implication of following this way is the subject of the next section. Its basic premise is that God reveals his sovereignty and supremacy more gloriously by sharing freedom with us than by withholding it from us.

Freedom in Christian Perspective

As our country's war on terrorism continues, many people I talk with express their concerns about safety and security with a common reference to "our way of life" and whether it can survive. When I ask what this phrase means to them especially, their answers invariably link "our way" with freedom and usually with being free from external constraints, for example:

> *Nobody should ever be able to tell us what we have to believe, think, or do. These things, we decide for ourselves.*
>
> *The people who founded our country came over here to get away from a government that intervened in everything and that eventually tried to keep our colonies here completely under its thumb. So we fought them off, and we've got to fight off anybody who tries to take our freedom away from us now.*
>
> *Freedom to me means being left alone just to be myself.*

Without a doubt, a vital part of what freedom is is freedom from undesirable impositions, such as from unjust laws, desiccated traditions, oppressive people and institutions, and indefensible ideologies. These freedoms are important enough for us to sacrifice even our lives to preserve them. However, freedom itself encompasses more than insulation from incursions that others inflict upon us. It also includes the power to act thoughtfully and purposefully on the basis of prior deliberation and choice. This latter is not freedom *from;* it is freedom *for.* It is freedom for the sake of exercising our responsibilities to ourselves, our neighbors, and God. Different as these two kinds of freedom are, their violation is nevertheless signaled in the same way: by guilt feelings. When we encroach unjustifiably on others or fail to act on the basis of principle, we commit wrongs for which we are guilty and for which we should feel guilty. Dealing responsibly with our guilt in these situations must include a commitment to the restoration of freedom in its fullness.

It is awe-inspiring to contemplate that the finite freedom with which God has endowed us is a measure of that very freedom that God himself exercises in choosing (1) to sustain an order of being other than himself at all and (2) to sustain this particular order of being rather than replace it with something else. Literally nothing in any way necessitated God's sharing this part of his own divine nature with us, just as nothing necessitated God's creating any world at all. He *chose* to create and to create in the way that he did and does. Two implications of this divine choosing are just as astonishing as the choices themselves.

First, by creating in us the capacity for principled actions that we are to determine for ourselves, and by calling us to develop that capacity as a condition for full partnership with him, God chose and still chooses to limit his power to act in the very order of things he lovingly sustains. Given this choice, and contrary to some of our most fervent expectations and demands, God not only does not, but also cannot, determine in advance that his creatures' every use of freedom will be as God wants it to be. God can and does communicate his intentions and desires for us clearly. In making his will known to us, God can and does invite, call, and even summon us to act in ways supportive of his plan for the whole of things. God can even choose to punish us when we do not. But what God cannot do, without compromising the fundamental nature of the world he has chosen to create, is abrogate our freedom by determining in advance our exercises of it.

Second, given the manifold ways that we trample not only others' freedom, but also our own, God's decision to share freedom with us must make him vulnerable to a degree of disappointment, anguish, sorrow, frustration, and anger that we can only begin to imagine. As parents, for example, we tend to focus our grief over ill-conceived and sometimes harmful acts primarily on our own and our children's wrongdoing. God, however, grieves over the errors of all humankind's ways. Because God does, the depth of his grieving must be almost unfathomable.

Must God subject himself to such suffering? God must if he remains committed to a world in which others besides himself have genuine freedom. Apart from such a commitment, the outrages that we human beings continue to inflict upon one another would surely warrant God's annihilation of our freedom altogether. Rather than hoarding the eternal completeness of his pure being, however, God has chosen to create others like God to share in it. With that decision, God takes upon himself the burden of preserving our freedom, even though our exercise of it so often goes awry. He does so because the kind of relationship he seeks with us is one based upon our freely chosen responses and not upon his overpowering and threatening commands.

God's great gift of freedom confronts us with a truly staggering range of possibilities. Just as God did not have to create us at all, we do not have to honor him for doing so. Just as God does not have to be mindful of us now, we do not have to be mindful of God, ever. Just as God could have chosen to create a world quite different from our own, we can choose to play different roles in the world that God did create from the roles that he wants us to play. Just as we can lift praise to the one true God who makes us fit for partnership with him, we can hunker down with a wholly abstract theology about a god who does everything for, to, and in place of us. Just as we can put our whole trust in Jesus Christ as God's decisive self-revelation and commit our lives to emptying ourselves for others, as God did, we can smugly conclude that nothing and no one is worth our ultimate trust and wallow contentedly in the nihilism of a risk-free, commitment-bare life. And just as we can seize freedom's power to incline our hearts ever more steadily toward the good, we can conscript that same power for self-serving purposes that compromise others' well-being, if not their very lives.

For most people, life veers constantly back and forth between all of these possibilities. It can seem like stumbling in the dark for any handhold at all or like being tossed about on the waves of a churning sea, and it can seem like racing on a clearly marked track with a goal in easy view. Life choices can be utterly clear one moment and hopelessly murky the next. For all of the uncertainty that attends the exercise of freedom, however, there is one choice that God forever bars from us: turning our backs on God, our neighbors, and the best that is in us with no feelings of guilt.

We can disguise our guilt feelings—even to the point of denying their reality altogether—at a verbal level. But we still know better. We still know, from the depths of our souls, that we are not what we are meant to be and, further, that we are the ones responsible for our shortcomings and the wrongdoing that is their origin. What we may know less well is that the very guilt that makes our wrongdoing "grievous unto us"—that makes us truly "miserable" offenders—is precisely what we need to feel in order to change the pattern of misusing our God-given freedom to a pattern reflective of God's highest hopes and dreams for us.

On Understanding Moral Evil, or Why We Misuse Our Freedom

Freedom as the power to determine beliefs and actions on the basis of careful deliberation and choice—the power of principled action—is one of the most misused of all God's gifts to us. Even if we have been mentored well in the art of using freedom wisely, it is still a constant struggle to think before we act, act for the right reasons only, and accept responsibility for the consequences of actions that do not turn out well. But unless we remain committed to the struggle, the forces that are everywhere aligned against peoples' becoming truly free will prevail, and the human community will have denied itself the glorious liberty that God intends everyone at all times and everywhere to enjoy in a community of worship and service. Why the struggle is so difficult is the subject of this concluding section. Its premise is that, in our present condition, it is easier to misuse freedom than it is to use it for good and that we misuse our freedom in two principal ways.

In the first place, we misuse the gift of freedom by refusing to use it at all. For some, the exercise of independent thinking and acting represents a dangerous path toward self-assertion at the expense of family stability, tribal and national unity, and social well-being in general. For others, the pursuit of principled action brings in its wake too much frustration, disappointment, danger, loss, and uncertainty to offset the satisfactions it affords. Both convictions lead to the same pattern of refusing to think for oneself, to take a stand, to risk others' misunderstanding and rejection, and, above all, to accept responsibility. These considerations remind us that freedom also includes the power not to decide what we will believe and do and the power to deny accountability for not deciding. However, if we use our freedom only to entertain idle thoughts about what we might like to do or should do, sometime, and never translate our ruminations into principled actions in the here and now, then we are not really free, no matter how secure we may be under others' protection, and no matter how prolific, heroic, or inspiring our imagined scenarios might be.

If we can misuse our God-given freedom by not using it at all, we can also misuse it to pursue relentlessly our own wants, needs, and goals at the expense of others. This second kind of misuse begins early, in the service of the "Me First/It's Mine" orientation of early childhood. It is because we do not know better when we are very young that we are not held strictly accountable for the misdeeds that flow from our unabashed self-centeredness. Given adequate nurture and guidance, though, most of us eventually become more attuned to and respectful of others' situations, rights, dignity, and intrinsic value and pursue our own interests in a less self-serving fashion as a result. Slowly, we learn to use our freedom more in the interest of doing what is right and less in the interest of doing what is wrong.

Why, however, given that God wants us to become truly free, is the path toward genuine freedom so narrow and so arduous for even very thoughtful and caring people to follow? The answer to this question is twofold. First, by the time we reach the age of accountability, we have already developed well-established patterns of using our freedom for purposes of self-aggrandizement. Second, it is always easier to repeat rather than to break from the kinds of things we have typically done in the past.

Whether from bullies on playgrounds or paramedics at accidents, from terrorists in caves or philanthropists in foundations, actions turn into habits that direct the expression of freedom with increasing consistency either to evil or to good. Unhappily, too many people become habituated to attending to their own needs and wants before or even in place of attending to others'. Worse still, there are always people around us—from hardened criminals to out-of-control psychopaths to self-ordained religious fanatics—who seem altogether incapable of doing anything other than pursue their warped objectives at the expense not only of others' well-being, but also of others' very existence on the earth.

Ancient Israel developed a profound and abiding understanding of how human beings can become so estranged from their original, God-endowed goodness: by habitually repeated evil actions, which eventually create a permanently imprinted "evil inclination":

> When the LORD saw how great was the wickedness of human beings on earth, and how their every thought and inclination were always wicked, he bitterly regretted that he had made mankind on earth. (Gen. 6:5-6 REB)

From Adam to Noah, the Old Testament's story of our origins tells us human beings' tediously repeated acts of disobedient, prideful self-assertion gradually eroded the spirit of gratitude and inner peace intended by God to lead them into fellowship and partnership with him. Seth's descendants could have reversed the process, but they did not. By the time of the Flood, the story goes on, God's disappointment with humanity reached a breaking point—but only temporarily. God promised Noah that he would never again lose all patience with human beings' abuses of their freedom.

The heart of these stories in the early chapters of Genesis is this: Though surely chagrined whenever anyone's evil inclination becomes harmful and infectious to others, God nevertheless remains committed to drawing even the most wayward into a loving embrace and partnership, constantly renewing in them, as in us, the original gift of the power to do good without canceling out the freedom to do the very evils he most abhors. The freedom to act as God desires us to act has never left and will never leave us; thus, we can still be held accountable for our actions, and we can still have fellowship with God that is chosen by us and not merely for us. However, we often exercise that freedom in ways not of God's choosing, and because we do, the inclination to follow "the devices and desires of our own hearts" has become stronger than the inclination to please God by following his will and way.

Christian theologians have often substituted for ancient Israel's understanding of evil inclination a doctrine of "original sin" that characterizes the human condition as utterly corrupt, by virtue of a loss of our capability to exercise our freedom in any other than evil ways. Our state of depravity, the doctrine has it, is one into which we are born, one that each generation transmits in its totality to the next, and one from which we can be redeemed by God alone, never by our own efforts. To the question of why we have such difficulty using our freedom wisely, this strand of the Christian tradition has a terribly simplistic answer: We cannot overcome the evil that has become inherent and permanent in all of humanity. Ancient Israel's answer is much better: It is hard to use freedom well because we are so out of the habit of using it well.

Throughout history, the evil inclination of human beings has unleashed consequences whose destructiveness defy calculation. Nevertheless, the inclination to evil can never, by itself, overwhelm the power in us to treat one another as God treats us: respectfully, compassionately, mercifully, and lovingly. Evil inclination is just that: an inclination, but not an irresistible urge to do evil. The inclination dictates behavior only when we allow it to do so in ourselves, and when we do not resist it in others.

Summary

By virtue of the power to act on principle rather than impulse, and to ensure that actions are chosen rather than coerced, human beings bear something of the very essence of God: freedom, like the freedom God exercises in fashioning a world with creatures capable of fellowship and partnership with him. God's decision to create us with a measure of his own freedom is at once glorious and fearsome. It is glorious in the invitation it contains to tend the created order lovingly in God's name. It is fearsome in the possibility it opens for untold evils to be brought about by freedom's misuse. That freedom can be misused, however, does not mean that it must be misused. What prevents the possibility from becoming a necessity is our God-given capacity to feel guilt when we misuse our freedom in the service of wrongdoing. The positive role that guilt feelings play in the restoration both of relationships alienated by our wrongdoing and of the capacity to use our freedom as God intends is the subject of the next chapter.

Chapter Three

Closing the Accounts on Remembered Wrongs

This chapter focuses on the process of achieving inner peace and reconciled relationships through taking our guilt and guilt feelings seriously enough to make amends for the harm we inflict. It is intended as a practical guide to healing relationships infected by our wrongdoing and experiencing fully the kind of life to which God calls us in Jesus Christ. The first section sketches just what this life is intended to be, by means of an exploration of a central theme in Pauline theology, the theme of peace through reconciliation.

On Becoming a Reconciled People

Of all the summary statements in the New Testament about how we are to live before God and others, one of the most powerful is Paul's assurance to his beloved and vexing congregation at Corinth: "God was in Christ reconciling the world to himself, no longer holding people's misdeeds against them, and has entrusted us with the message of reconciliation" (2 Cor. 5:19 REB). Immediately preceding these words, Paul suggested that God's message of reconciliation is the basis of a comprehensive ministry of reconciliation to others. Clearly, for Paul, "reconciliation" is a key word for understanding the foundation of both Christian existence in the world and Christian ministry everywhere.

Closely associated in Paul's mind with reconciliation is peacemaking, an overcoming of enmity toward ourselves, between people, and among people and God. The ultimate source of the enmity is human wrongdoing. Sometimes, Paul writes about wrongdoing in the strict sense of wrongful actions, such as misdeeds or trespasses or sins. When wrongdoing is so construed, what is basically wrong with us as human beings—what creates most of the enmity that is so pervasive among us—is that we do not do what God asks of us. But there is more involved than this.

For Paul, human wrongdoing is manifest at a level deeper than just our actions, at a level that our faith tradition often refers to as faults, for example: "Spare thou those, O God, who confess their faults." This petition from Eucharistic liturgy speaks, as did Paul, less about actions of the moment and more about long-standing traits, attitudes, dispositions, and weaknesses of character. From this perspective, our problems with ourselves, one another, and God are not only about what we do and do not do; they are about what we are. As Paul experienced it, God's call to the ministry of reconciliation—peacemaking—is a conferring of power to overcome not only the destructive effects of our actions, but also the degraded condition of our very being. In Christ, we are new creations (2 Cor. 5:17).

Reconciliation, then, involves not only changes in how we act toward ourselves, others, and God. It also involves a transformation of our very being. In either sense, reconciliation is both an ideal and a process. As an ideal, reconciliation expresses an enduring union between people who have found their own best selves, who have set aside their mutual differences, and who with one accord serve God and savor God's presence among them. By holding the ideal firmly before us, we can be contributors rather than hindrances to its realization.

As a process rather than an end-state, reconciliation begins with God's coming in love rather than judgment, gathers energy from our acknowledgment of guilt, and spurs us steadily in the direction of our loving ourselves and others as God loves us. Two things about this process especially interested Paul. First, God's reconciling work in the world is a work of love on his part, and not of merit on ours. If God were to measure his actions toward us only by what we deserve, our wrongdoing would merit only his anger, contempt, and punishment. Second, the love with which God initiates the process is, paradoxically, both independent of and dependent upon human response.

On the one hand, God's decision no longer to count our wrongdoing against us is an act of sheer grace that flows from an all-surpassing love that nothing in all creation can limit, contain, or impede. Even if we remain indifferent to, disbelieving of, or even contemptuous of God's manifold mercies, these mercies will continue. On the other hand, though the initiation of the process of reconciliation is independent of human response, the fulfillment of the process is not. It depends on our choosing to become a reunited people ourselves, serving God as agents of reunion to all humankind. As the previous chapter pointed out, we have the God-given capacity not to make this choice. Exercising the capacity in this way, though, will mean that we will miss our true destiny in the world and, with it, the greatest joy that God can provide us.

Given what is at stake in choosing between the paths of reconciliation or self-serving, are we left wholly to our own devices in making the choice? Is there nothing that might, without predetermining our choice, at least incline us in the direction that

God wants us to follow? In Paul and the Christian tradition as a whole, there are two basic answers to these questions. One answer is that God inspires us to make the right choice by assuring us inwardly of his love for us and his forgiveness of our sins: "The Spirit of God affirms to our spirit that we are God's children" (Rom. 8:16 REB). Those who find this answer compelling usually insist that only by experiencing God's reconciliation in our hearts personally can we truly choose and follow the way of reconciliation. Holding a belief about reconciliation only in our minds will never suffice.

One major problem with this first answer is that it anchors our relationship with God not in God's love for us, but in having just the right experience of that love. The other major problem is that the answer does not speak to everyone equally. Many people, professed Christians included, never experience a personal encounter with God of the sort Paul describes above and yet live morally and spiritually exemplary lives. Are we to say that their faith is less genuine than the faith of those who have had the requisite experience?

The other answer to our questions about what can prompt us to use our freedom wisely, and choose for ourselves the pattern of life that God wants us to choose, is the answer to which much of this book has already been pointing: our God-given capacity to feel guilty in response to the awareness of being guilty. Not everyone can claim to have experienced "the assurance of the Spirit." But all of us, "like sheep, have gone astray." Unlike sheep, however, we know that we have done so, we share in common a sense of guilt about doing so, and we have at our disposal the means to become the people we need to be in order to share God's ministry of reconciliation to the world. The next sections of this chapter discuss how we can put our guilt at the service of making peace with ourselves, with one another, and between ourselves and God.

What Guilt Feelings Are Made Of

Some people do not permit their conscience to mean much to them. For most of us, however, the pain of guilt and the pressure to make amends pulsate steadily within us, even reaching into our sleep to produce disturbing dreams and debilitating agitation. By "guilt" here is meant a state or condition of indebtedness to another or others because of things we have done or left undone, whose result is offense or harm. In this sense of the term, being guilty means being under an obligation to make right an offensive or hurtful act or pattern of such acts. It means being under an obligation to do something to offset or compensate for our wrongdoing, by (a) acknowledging both the wrongs we commit and the weaknesses within us that lead us to commit them, (b) making it up in some acceptable way to those we offend or harm, and (c) consciously working to change our patterns of behavior that bring about the undesirable acts in the first place.

Whenever we become aware that we have done something offensive or harmful either to ourselves or to someone else, we normally feel some combination of fear, regret, and remorse. We have these feelings whether our actions and their consequences were intended or not, and whether the feelings themselves are generated by us or evoked in us by others. The intensity of our feelings is usually proportional to the degree to which the persons we have offended or harmed matter to us in some way. For example, we might feel a slight twinge of regret for momentary rudeness to a store clerk, but we are likely to forget about both the rudeness and the regret rather quickly because the encounter with that particular person was fleeting and unlikely to recur. By contrast, we might be utterly unable to get out of our minds a flippant remark to a close friend, that we never thought would be taken personally, even when our friend repeatedly tells us to forget about it.

The components of fear and regret in guilt feelings have to do primarily with anticipated retaliation or punishment for our actions or with loss of a relationship, for example:

> *You just wait until your father gets home!*

> *Somehow I seem to find a way to sabotage myself at every step of the way toward recovery. Here I make it to four*

months without a drink and then go on a bender. I don't want to go home, for fear of what my family is going to think and say. And if the boss finds out, I'll be fired for sure.

As one of her friends, I think I have an obligation to tell her about her husband's affair, but if I do, I'm afraid she'll never speak to me again. This whole thing is just tearing me up inside.

All of these statements exhibit a blending of nervous anticipation with feeling sorry for having done or not done something.

Fear and regret are powerful inducements to dealing with our wrongdoing. It can be painful to admit offending or hurting someone, just as it can be inconvenient to "work it out" with the one we have wronged, and just as it can be arduous to change ourselves for the better in the process. However, the pain, inconvenience, and arduousness are still easier to endure than living in a perpetual state of regretful worry about ourselves or about the state of a relationship, or than distancing ourselves from relationships to keep our worry at bay. For example, the young man doomed to await his father's arrival and castigation also allowed his fear and regret, aroused by an angry mother, to do its proper work. While contemplating his fate, he said to a friend: *It's gonna kill me to look my dad in the eye and tell him I broke his best fishing rod, but I'd better do it or Mom will tell him first.*

Even though feelings of fear and regret can motivate us to take responsibility for the hurts we cause others, they focus on our own concerns more than on the well-being of the persons we have wronged. The less self-serving element in our guilt feelings is remorse: genuine sorrow for our wrongdoing, whose source is respect for others' rights, for our own, and for the sacred worth and dignity of others and ourselves as creatures of God. Remorseful guilt, in contrast with merely anxious or regretful guilt, arises in the context of relationships with people we care about for themselves and not for what they do for us. If our relationship with another is based primarily on what we get out of it personally, harming the relationship in some way may arouse fear and regret in us, but not remorse. If, however, the relationship is one of mutual affection and love, awareness that we have harmed it almost certainly will stir in us feelings of sadness for what we have done, along with concern to do whatever we can to rectify the situation.

More reliably than do fear and regret, remorse can lead to amends-making and personal transformation based upon respecting what others need rather than upon calculating what we need to do in order to keep getting what we want from them. Being "heartily sorry for these our misdoings" serves the interests of reconciliation far better than merely being fearful of their consequences or wishing that we had not committed the wrongful acts in the first place. To be sure, remorse, too, can be self-serving. As do fear and regret, remorse can provoke us to take action aimed at ridding ourselves of the pain of the feeling itself, whether or not our actions address the needs of those we have hurt. One example of such self-serving remorse is foisting an apology upon someone we have hurt before he or she is ready or able to hear it from us. However, in spite of the fact that remorse can take an unwanted direction from time to time, its primary thrust is toward restoration in broken relationships and maturation in those whose wrongdoing creates the brokenness. Anxious and regretful guilt is content with putting things back on an even keel, whether or not the condition of an injured party is helped much in the process. Remorseful guilt, by contrast, pushes us to change both what we do and what we are, ultimately for the betterment of all whom we wrong.

Getting Beyond Feeling Guilty: The Next Steps

Clearly, we cannot hope to restore relationships threatened or broken by our wrongdoing unless we acknowledge to ourselves what we have done, and what we have become, to those we hurt. Acknowledgment is the absolutely essential first step, difficult as it is to take. Even so, it is still only that: a first step. More important steps are yet to come, especially the steps of apologizing and making amends. Neither of these steps is any easier than the first one.

Whether by means of words, facial expression, or gestures, it is relatively easy to express "I'm sorry" to someone. Meaning what is expressed is another matter. The number of perfunctory apologies all of us have received—and offered as well—bears eloquent testimony to how hard it can be to get beyond admitting only to ourselves the hurts we inflict and to take genuine responsibility for them before others. If the hurts are ever to be healed, though, acknowledging them must be followed by apologizing for them and expressing a willingness to be accountable for them. Sadly, however, rather than facilitating the taking of responsibility, proffering an apology can also be a way of avoiding it, for example:

> *All right, all right, I'm sorry! There! Is that enough for you?*
>
> *Look, I'm not happy I let that go on for so long. But let's just put it behind us and move ahead, OK? It's not really something for you to get so upset about.*
>
> *Oops! Guess I should've gotten these figures to you before this. You won't believe how busy I've been.*

Just as apologies can be compromised by insincerity, they can be nullified by excuses. Even very trusting and compassionate people feel their patience challenged when apologies come smothered in self-defense. What we really want to hear in an apology are words like these:

> *Much as I hate to admit it, I'm the one who said it, and I had no business saying it. I was way out of line, and I'm ready to apologize to everyone who heard me say what I said.*
>
> *You're right. My hot temper is giving everybody in the office grief, and I have to start working on it. I am going to start*

working on it. One way you can help me is by being as honest with me as you've just been.

I don't have the words to tell you right now how sorry I am for being such a poor friend these last months. You've been dealing with so much, and I could have been there with you but wasn't. I'm looking pretty hard at things these days, not to rationalize, but to figure out how to get back what I've lost in myself. Is there anything I can do here and now that might begin to make things better between us? I'm ready to do it.

Instead of words like these, what we often get by way of apologies is self-justification, for example: *I'm sure this looks bad, but just let me tell you what I was trying to do by giving the job to Steve without asking you first.* We ought not to be wholly surprised by such responses as this. One root meaning for the word "apology," from ancient Greek times to the present, is "defense": a credible, positive account of how and why people do the kinds of things they do and are the kinds of people they are. Plato wrote one of his most treasured dialogues to provide an apology for the life and calling of Socrates, not to provide us reasons for excusing his mentor's mistakes, but to demonstrate why we should revere him as a great teacher. In the New Testament, all four Gospels render a similar kind of apology for the life and ministry of our Lord, here in the form of defending his messianic identity in spite of the fact that he was rejected by most of his own people and died like a common criminal. In the light of this long and important history of the word "apology," we should make at least a little room for apologies that offer more justifications than regrets, that highlight virtue, good intentions, and righteousness more than flaws, thoughtlessness, and egoism.

Just how much room we should make for the element of self-defense in others' apologies depends largely upon whether those who incorporate it are also the kinds of people who generally hold themselves accountable for their actions. It may be that by remaining open to understanding the reasons for someone's behavior, even when the behavior has proved offensive or harmful to us, we can make a significant contribution of our own to letting an apology do its proper work. Consider, by way of examples, the following expressions of regret and remorse:

> *I made a really bad call not telling you what your sister was saying behind your back, and I'm truly sorry. At the time, it seemed to me that you had all you could handle dealing with ———'s problems and that you didn't need anything else to bother you. But that was a judgment that I didn't have the right to make. I promise never to do it again.*

> *I believed with all my heart that God wanted me to be a pastor, and I just didn't listen to people who were gently guiding me to take a second look at what I thought I experienced as a call. As you know all too well, I made a mess of the two churches I was asked to serve. But God didn't give up on me; he's showing me how to be a good Christian in a parish without my having to be the leader of it. How grateful I am to all of you who have been so patient with me through all this.*

Though different in content and tone, these two statements have several important characteristics in common. They convey genuine regret and remorse. They offer reasons but contain no excuses intended to get their perpetrators "off the hook." They are forward-looking, expressing hope for both restoration and improvement in the relationships that occasion them. Together, they demonstrate clearly the difference between healthy apologies and lame excuses. They model for us how to move from acknowledgment, through apology, to the third step of dealing constructively with our guilt: making amends.

Sometimes, making amends in a relationship is relatively simple. Jack damages the lawnmower he has borrowed from his neighbor Andy. He gets it fixed and returns it. Andy pronounces it "good as new." Marge forgets to order the tickets she promised her daughter, Cindy, for the opening of an exciting new play. With some scurrying around, she finds two tickets for another performance, and she and Cindy have a thoroughly enjoyable evening together. Bill borrows one of his professor's favorite books and loses it. He buys a new copy for the professor the next day. In all three of these cases, a momentary disruption to a relationship is overcome; the relationship is restored almost exactly to its prior condition. A lawnmower works again; a play delights; a book is returned to its proper place on a shelf.

Making amends is usually more complicated than this. More frequently, we would find that Andy's lawnmower cannot be fixed, that the play concludes its run with no seats becoming available, and that the professor's favorite book turns out to be filled with his own marginal notes. If Jack, Marge, and Bill were faced with these circumstances, they probably would respond, respectively, by finding another lawnmower, buying tickets to a different play, and adding to the new copy of the much used book some other things that the professor might appreciate. Andy, Cindy, and the professor would be compensated for their respective losses; but, to varying degrees, they still would not be able to enjoy what they enjoyed before. They would have to make do with a substitute for what cannot be given them directly.

Most amends-making, of necessity, is substitutionary in character. For what we cannot recover, replace, or undo, we substitute something else, including a new covenant for old promises and cheerful acceptance of greater responsibilities for running away from lesser ones. These kinds of amends offer more than a mere turning back of the clock. Instead, they offer to relationships jeopardized by carelessness a higher level of attentiveness, respectfulness, and possibility—at least, if the substitutions they propose are adequate in the eyes of those who suffer the original offenses. Only the injured parties can finally determine whether their relationships with those who have wronged them will be allowed to "mend" by their wrongdoers' efforts at making "amends." In the following examples, the process of amends-making yielded mutually rewarding outcomes:

> *I'm really sorry I didn't come by yesterday when I said I would. Can I make it up to you by buying lunch today?*

> *It's really bothering me that I've missed so many of this committee's meetings this year. Tell you what: I'll take on chairing the project that we always have to dragoon someone into doing, and I'll take it on cheerfully. Would this be a fair deal?*
>
> *The dish I broke isn't replaceable, and I know how much it hurts to lose something that's been in your family for so long. So here's my idea: let me replace it with whatever you pick that's close to it, and then let me do some things around the house that are your least favorite things to do yourself.*

Sometimes, no matter how hard we try to "make things right" with people we hurt, our efforts fail. Two obvious reasons for our failures, of course, are (a) insincerity in our apologies and (b) failure to do what we said we would do to rectify the particular situations. Given, though, that we have fully acknowledged our wrongdoing and made more than reasonable offers of amends, we must look elsewhere for an understanding of why reconciliation is still far off. One place to look is in the direction of the personhood of those we have wronged. The other is in the direction of the wrongs we have done to them.

Once, a friend shared with me his anguish over an impending breakup with his fiancée. *I learned too late*, he said, *that she took personally a couple of not-so-flattering things I once tossed off about her son's rudeness*. When I expressed curiosity about how that could have put a whole relationship at risk, my friend replied:

> *That was only the tip of a very large iceberg. I love ——— more than there are words for, but the hard truth is that she's the kind of person who looks for the slightest hint of another's criticism, and once she picks it up, she goes into hyper-alert and just waits for more. She started keeping score on me, and no matter how hard I weighed what I said to her, I just seemed to keep on saying the wrong thing.*

Painful as this relationship was for my friend, his fiancée's ending it was even more distressing to him. Months after the breakup, he told me about a "revelation" that came to him the night before:

> *All of a sudden it dawned on me that if our relationship really had been solid, we'd have found a way to share our thoughts and feelings better without reading too much into the way we expressed them. Our not doing so just meant that we shouldn't be together.*

Though my friend's revelation oversimplified his relationship somewhat, it helped him move on from it without nagging recriminations and kept before him a very important truth about all relationships: No matter how much we might want it to be otherwise, some people may never give us the opportunity to repair the damage we do them, usually because of unresolved issues that plague them from old relationships and old agendas. Either they are unable to tolerate another's mistakes at all, or they are unable to accept the normal kinds of substitutionary acts that are intended to make up for them. They cannot seem to let go of the wrongs we do them, no matter what.

There is another reason that people may close us out of their lives for hurting them: The hurt that we do them is too painful for them to transcend, and too great for us to compensate. For months now, Hal has been spending many of his waking hours sitting in a den chair, talking and moving very little, inconsolable. The day after Christmas, coming home with his wife from an afternoon of bargain-hunting, he was unable to stop his car in time to avoid hitting his neighbors' two-year-old, who, without warning, ran into his path. The child died under the wheels. That Hal had not been drinking, that he jammed on his brakes, that he swerved as sharply as he could, have made no difference to him; he is overcome with grief and self-blame, even as his neighbors, the child's parents, are drowning in grief and anger.

In a situation like this, it is difficult to envision what "making amends" could possibly mean. Here, reconciliation will require something quite different from anything that we have been discussing in this present chapter. Acknowledgment, apology, and a sincere attempt to make amends are essential. But they will not be enough. Nothing that Hal can ever do will bring back the dead child; nothing that Hal can ever do will fully assuage his neighbors' agony over losing their daughter, his good intentions notwithstanding. For closing this kind of account, only forgiveness will suffice. Eventually, Hal's neighbor will have to forgive him, and Hal will have to forgive himself, precisely because nothing else will bring healing to their own relationship.

Just what forgiveness can mean in situations such as Hal's, and how forgiveness is possible in any kind of situation, will be the subject of later chapters. Before we turn to that subject, however, there is still more to explore about guilt itself, in specific, about (a) guilt that we have but do not acknowledge and (b) guilt that we acknowledge but do not really have. The first is often referred to as "unconscious guilt." As the next chapter will show, though this way of looking at the matter is popular in some psychological circles, it is a difficult perspective to reconcile with faith's understanding of who and what we are in God's sight. The second kind of guilt is sometimes referred to as "neurotic," or as "false" guilt. As we will see, it is more accurate to speak of this kind of guilt simply as a feeling without a basis in fact. With respect to both kinds of guilt, the fundamental point is that we must deal with them, too, if we are truly to close the accounts on our accumulated guilt.

Summary

Because we do know how we should live before God, and because we have a measure of God's own freedom to decide whether or not we will live in accordance with the best that we know, we alone bear the responsibility for the decisions that we make about our lives and relationships. As it did for ancient Israel and for Christians in times past, Deuteronomy 30:15 expresses these truths succinctly and completely for us, too: "Today I offer you the choice of life and good, or death and evil"

(REB). Wrong choices, those that fly in the face of our own and others' best interests as members of God's own household, put us in a condition of obligation—of guilt—toward whomever we offend or harm by means of them. Our condition of being guilty is, by God's grace, signaled in us by feeling guilty. Guilt feelings—fear, regret, and remorse—are intended to lead us to reparative actions through a process of acknowledgment, apology, and making amends, to the end that alienation within ourselves, between ourselves and others, and ultimately between humankind and God, is gathered into God's ongoing work, in Christ, of reconciling all things to himself.

CHAPTER FOUR

FROM GUILT WE KNOW NOT, AND FROM GUILT WE HAVE NOT, GOOD LORD DELIVER US

In the previous chapter, we looked at guilt typically experienced in some combination of fear, regret, and remorse. We deal with it by owning up to our wrongdoing, apologizing for it, and rectifying the situations we create by it. Sometimes, the first step of owning up is the hardest, and, rather than take it, we push the guilt that we have and feel as far from awareness as possible, for example: *How could they possibly think I would do something like that?* Other times, the second and third steps are the more painful ones, and, rather than climb them, we depend on making our apologies so winsome that the people we hurt will let us off the hook, for example: *Now don't you worry another minute about this. I know you didn't mean to do it. All is forgiven.*

Below the surface of these easily recognized strategies of not dealing with guilt lie two patterns, often unacknowledged, that can do serious damage to our moral and spiritual integrity and growth. The first is a pattern of continuous, rather than occasional, denial either that we are feeling guilty, we are guilty, or both. Modern psychology frequently refers to this pattern as one of "repressing" our guilt, in the sense of making it as inaccessible as possible to reflection and modification. The sections to follow will show how we can deal with out-of-awareness guilt without appealing to theories of the unconscious psyche that pastors and lay caregivers neither have nor need to have at their disposal.

The second pattern of chronic failure to deal adequately with guilt is a pattern of overvaluing minor offenses, confusing real transgressions with imagined ones, and losing objectivity about what we are and are not accountable for. In pastoral practice, this pattern is most often spoken of as a pattern of being overly scrupulous. Modern psychology once referred to the guilt that the pattern produces as "neurotic" guilt. In the sections to follow, both the pattern and the guilt are discussed in terms of guilt that we feel but do not really have.

Surely It's Someone Else's Fault

One way to avoid dealing responsibly with guilt is to make ourselves oblivious both to the guilt itself and to the uncomfortable feelings that the awareness of it arouses. As the following vignette illustrates, the self-serving quality of this strategy is usually transparent to others before it is to us.

At a party, Martha disparages the homemaking skills of her sister, Ellen, to a mutual friend: *If you think your house is a disaster area, wait until you see Ellen's!* The next day, Ellen shares with Martha how much her feelings were hurt when she found out what Martha said. Martha replies tersely: *Oh, you know I didn't mean anything by it. Don't be so sensitive.* Surprised over the expression on Ellen's face, Martha blurts out: *Well, okay, I'm sorry. Can you let it go now?* As the next exchange indicates, Martha's response has not helped the situation:

> *Ellen: Martha, are you aware of how many times you come out with something before you think about it, and then wonder why people get irritated with you?*
> *Martha: Ellen, I said I was sorry! What more do you want? Come on!*

Now, Ellen is angry, Martha is defensive, and the two are at an impasse. What makes the situation especially frustrating for Ellen is knowing that her sister is capable of so much more than the insensitivity she shows to her ill-considered statements' effect on others. By nature, Ellen knows, Martha is a caring person who goes out of her way to be helpful and supportive in most of her relationships, in spite of the fact that many of her friends refer to her, with mild irritation, as "the woman who'll never admit doing anything wrong." Most of Martha's friends see only obstinacy in her refusal to acknowledge hurting someone. Ellen knows Martha better, as sometimes only a sister can.

As irritated as Ellen is with her sister, she also understands that denying responsibility, blaming others, offering only superficial apologies, and demanding that others accept them as if they were sincerely rendered are all ways that Martha uses to mask the intense fear and regret that she feels when, deep down, she knows that she has said or done something to hurt someone. Frustrated over her inability to express her insights to Martha constructively, Ellen years ago opted for an indirect approach with their mutual friends, expressing her resentment as open-mindedness, for example: *Oh, I never pay any attention to Martha when she talks that way; she says things like that to all her friends.*

Most people who are as caring as Martha strives to be eventually find that covering over guilt and the feeling of it no longer fools anyone. It took Martha an especially long time to make this discovery in her own case, but she finally did make it and sought help. First, she confessed to her priest her many refusals to admit and take responsibility for hurting others' feelings and then, with his blessing, began meeting with an experienced lay caregiver, Brenda, from her parish whom she knows and respects. The church in which Martha and Brenda have been active for many years represents a tradition that affirms the distinctive role and responsibility of the clergy for helping people deal with guilt through confessing sins, doing penance, and receiving absolution. Brenda affirms their church's practice, respects their priest as Martha's primary confessor, and confines her own ministry with Martha to active, empathic listening and refraining from offering interpretations or passing judgment of any kind. As a result, Martha has come to share more and more about what she calls her "nagging conscience" and her desperate efforts to protect herself against it by denying her uncaring acts and blaming others for being oversensitive. She is beginning to acknowledge her imperfections without becoming overwhelmed by them and, in the process, is more open to accepting and dealing with others' legitimate criticisms, instead of denying their validity out of hand.

Whenever the anticipation of having to acknowledge guilt begins to cause us distress, it can be tempting just to ignore being and feeling guilty altogether. However, we cannot exorcise unpleasant realities permanently merely by refusing them entrance into our awareness. All we will accomplish by denying our guilt—or anything else that is true about us—is a loss of vital energy from trying harder and harder to convince ourselves that what others see plainly in us is not there. The better approach is to take a hard look at why we often choose to avoid rather than confront the guilt that we plainly bear and deeply feel. The next three sections of this chapter identify and discuss three explanations for denying the guilt and guilt feelings that others so easily see.

When Present Realities Are Only Painful Reminders

In the middle of a discussion about how to get their two children to three different activities the next afternoon, Cheryl suddenly shouted out to her husband, Larry:

> *I can't take even one more criticism from you! I just can't! If you so much as look at me the wrong way, I'll go upstairs and hide out for the rest of the night, and you can figure out what to do about the kids all by yourself.*

Later, as Larry recalled the scene to a close friend, he remarked:

> *It's like this a lot between Cheryl and me, and always has been. No matter how careful I try to be, I usually find some way to set her off, and I feel terrible when I do. If it isn't something I say or don't say, it's a look on my face or not sitting close enough to her or—just anything, I guess.*

Larry's friend, who has known both Larry and Cheryl since childhood, offered a helpful appraisal of the situation:

> *Larry, we all say and do things sometimes that get things in an uproar. Goodness only knows how often I do. But you're talking about Cheryl's making mountains out of molehills, and, yes, she sure can. Maybe it'll help, though, to think again about what it was like for her growing up the way she did. Can't you still hear her folks yelling and yelling and yelling at her, all the time, and never giving her a break? You had it easy, old buddy, but Cheryl's family was just like mine, so she and I used to commiserate a lot. I guess we both grew up seeing criticism everywhere, whether it was there or not.*

Happily, Cheryl and Larry eventually came to terms with the effect their respective upbringings had on their marriage and used what they learned from their struggles to make significant improvements in their enjoyment of each other. Cheryl in particular has something important to teach us about why we sometimes push as far from our awareness as we can even the possibility that we might be guilty of something: We "can't take even one more criticism." In the particular situation just described, Cheryl was not guilty of anything. Neither was Larry. They were simply overwhelmed, momentarily, by honestly made commitments that they did not know how they could fulfill. Cheryl, however, became immobilized by criticism she thought she heard, that Larry did not make, because she was flooded by too many memories of too many criticisms that too many other people in her life did make, unjustifiably, long before she could stand up for herself.

Childhood experiences of being judged too harshly, of being found wanting by the people that we care about the most, can drive any of us to avoid "even one more criticism" at almost any cost. Vulnerable and dependent, young children have little option but to accept the criticisms heaped upon them by the powerful caregivers in their lives, whether those criticisms are fairly based, have a constructive intent, express underlying love, or not. Long before a child is able to assess others' judgments objectively by means of the God-given capacity to know oneself truly, his or her self-image is already held captive by the gaze of abusive family members who inflict their own self-loathing on those to whom they reluctantly give birth. The malignant messages of such people to their ill-fated offspring can be permanently crippling:

Can't you ever do anything right?

You're acting just like that no-good father of yours.

You're never going to amount to anything.

Some people come into the world with enough innate resilience to survive even the most extreme kinds of criticism. Others only partially recover from the emotional and spiritual depletion that criticism sets in motion early in life. Still others, those about whom this section is especially concerned, survive the nurturing failures of their primary caregivers by avoiding and denying criticism at every stage of their adult lives. Unfortunately, their strategy leaves them closed off to the things they do that really are offensive or harmful to others. Because their (denied) negative self-image is already like an open wound, admitting to even more wrongdoing is like rubbing a caustic substance into it. Rather than bear the pain of confronting yet another failure, they first try to deny what they do altogether or put the blame on others. If these ploys do not work, they then plead some version of incapacitation to escape responsibility or reprisal, to the effect: *You can't blame me for this; I never was taught any better.*

Tragically, people who really do suffer from terrible childhoods have difficulty even hearing, much less understanding and appreciating, words that members of healthier families take for granted, such as:

> *Sure you can do it better, but just look how far you've come already!*
>
> *Of all the wonderful things that have happened in our lives, nothing is more wonderful than your being born.*
>
> *There's nothing that you could ever say or do that could make us stop loving you.*

Coming into adulthood with crushing burdens of others' discounts, criticism, and blame sometimes leads to relinquishing the possibility of ever hearing an encouraging word for oneself, even when just such an encouraging word is there for the listening. It can also lead to a desperate foraging under the tables of even the most manipulative people for the smallest crumbs of kindness and affection, at whatever cost to one's dignity in the moment and one's prospects for the future. Compared with these two alternatives, refusing to admit to wrongdoing may seem the healthier course.

On Not Letting People Matter Enough

A second explanation for some people's denying guilt is that they do not believe that other people are worth caring much about, if at all. Holding firmly to this belief, and supporting it by a selective attention that remembers only the ill-temperedness and not the good intentions and will of others, leads almost inevitably not to allowing ourselves to feel the appropriate concern whenever something that we do results in harm to someone else. At the most malignant stage of this studied indifference, we stop letting other people matter to us enough to hurt for them at all when we do hurt them.

Not long ago, a friend of mine surprised me with what, for him, was a singularly unfeeling comment about not calling a coworker whose mother had taken ill: *But, hey, no big deal.* If that were really true, I asked myself, I wonder why my friend is bringing the incident up at all. When I shared my question with him, he replied: *Oh, oh. You know, this thing must be bothering me more than I want to admit to myself.* Now, I thought, my friend is back on track; both his coworker and his coworker's feelings obviously do matter to him, and he's letting himself know that they do. Rather than continue to play down the significance of his forgetfulness, my friend begged off further conversation with me in order to find his coworker and to apologize for his callousness.

How much my friend treasures his coworker and the relationship they have together is not appreciated at all by one acquaintance of both, Jack, for whom getting close to people—indeed, to anyone—is singularly uncomfortable. As Jack puts it, *What's the percentage in getting that involved with anybody, on the job or anywhere? All you get for it is a lot of hassle.* Not surprising is that, most people who know this man describe him as someone "who couldn't care less about anything or anybody except himself." His younger brother has a little different perspective:

> *Yeah, Jack is pretty hard to take sometimes. No matter what you do to reach out to him, you just don't get much back. But I'll tell you a little secret. The reason he won't get close to people is that he's scared to. He's been burned a lot in his life—a lot more than I have—and he's just too afraid it'll happen again.*

If we do not admit to ourselves just how much someone matters to us, and then do something that is offensive or harmful to that person, we likely will notice neither what we have done nor the guilt that we feel over what we have done. In my friend's case, the obliviousness was only momentary because he does care about people, genuinely and deeply. In Jack's case, however, the stress that his uncaring puts on relationships is much more serious. Jack is plagued by a constant, global apprehension that getting close to anyone will result in the loss of his independence. Armoring himself against dependency and the fear of it by avoiding strong emotional attachments, he has cultivated a deep forgetfulness of his God-given capacity to feel remorse. Like Jack, many people work very hard to convince themselves not to let others matter to them very much, and as a result they inflict considerable unhappiness on those naive enough still to love and care about them.

People who are in denial about how much they need others' concern and friendship, or about how much others mean to them, do not do well when confronted by the hurt of those whom they themselves have hurt. Most typically, they try to minimize the seriousness of the situation as, for instance, my friend did for a moment: *No big deal.* If the aggrieved party does not go away quietly, the offenders get vocally angry and begin shifting blame to the very persons they have wounded, for example: *Now you're beginning to make me mad. I can't believe you're making so much out of such a minor incident. What's wrong with you?* In the twinkling of an eye, they deform their victims into malevolent persecutors. Instead of apology and amends, they offer only more criticism, all the while mistaking their own fall into a slough of thoughtlessness, irresponsibility, and unassuageable loneliness for a guilt trip cruelly and without cause imposed on them by someone else.

Keeping Up Appearances at All Costs

Along with pushed-aside memories of judgment and condemnation from childhood and the fear of letting people matter enough to feel guilt when we hurt them, there is a third explanation for habitually denying guilt and guilt feelings: the need to be seen by others at our best. For some people, fulfilling this very normal need consumes a disproportionate amount of life energy. The image they project becomes as important as the reality behind it, and sometimes even more so. Since what they most want others to see in them is responsibility, rectitude, and righteousness, having to admit to anything that even remotely resembles thoughtlessness, wrongfulness, and waywardness can provoke serious inner turmoil.

When image becomes this important to us, the slightest hint that anything we do might be received less than positively typically elicits the kind of denial that has been the primary subject of the previous two sections. At the extreme, we refuse to consider even the possibility that some people choose to look upon us less than favorably, no matter how irritatingly we act toward them, for example:

> *He'll come around; he really looks forward to all my visits, even though he doesn't show it sometimes. I'm just gonna keep on showing up and telling him about the Lord and praying with him because that's what Jesus wants me to do.*

> *Yes, it does bother me sometimes not to get a lot of appreciation for what I'm trying to do for this firm, especially when I get so many criticisms that don't have any basis in fact. But eventually, everybody will see that I've been right all along. They really know it now but just don't want to admit it.*

> *A lot of people have a hard time giving compliments when compliments are due, and I just have to be patient with them.*

Denial can also take the form of rejecting any and every notion that we might have something to apologize for, to repent of, or to be ashamed about, for example:

> *I can forgive you for being so angry with me because I know I didn't do anything to deserve it.*
>
> *Certainly I can't claim to be perfect. Only Jesus can claim that. But all my life, I've tried to be a good Christian and resisted every one of the world's temptations. When the day comes to give an account of how I've lived, I won't have any worries, and I'm praying that you won't either.*
>
> *Even though you think I haven't kept my pledge to you, please trust me when I say that I've never worked harder at anything in my life as I have honoring our agreement and that I'm not the kind of person who ever goes back on his word.*

All three of these lofty statements proved convincing to their respective hearers. However, in spite of the high-mindedness of those who uttered them, each exudes something less noble: a preoccupation with maintaining a certain image in the eyes of others, along with a steadfastness in resisting any suggestion that they might do anything in conflict with that image.

It's All My Fault

To this point in the chapter, the focus has been on guilt that we have but do not allow ourselves to feel, and on why we choose to deal with real guilt by denying it. Now, we turn to another approach to guilt altogether: holding onto guilt feelings, either about offenses that are less significant than we assess them to be or about offenses that we have not in fact committed. Nowadays, it is fashionable to speak of both kinds of feelings in terms of "false guilt." There is something to be said for such a characterization. Feeling more guilt than a situation actually calls for, or any guilt at all when we have done nothing wrong, strongly suggests that at least some of our guilt abides more in our imagination than in objective reality.

The principal problem with the notion of false guilt is that it does not do justice to the felt reality of guilt, even when the feeling itself has little or no basis in fact. The feeling can be very real to us, whether or not we have committed an offense about which we ought to feel guilty. Because this is so, we cannot hope to deal with so-called false guilt adequately unless we first respect its manifest power over us. Certainly we will help neither ourselves nor anyone else deal with guilt feelings by cavalier remarks such as *You've got nothing to feel guilty about; get over it!*

A better way to speak about the kinds of guilt presently under discussion is to substitute for "false" guilt the characterization "unrealistic" guilt. As the following brief descriptions show, people can experience very real feelings of guilt even when the guilt they feel is unrealistic in the context it appears:

> *In midevening, Millie suddenly realizes that it is Mother's Day and that she has not yet called her mother. She immediately goes to the phone, places the call, and has a strained conversation. Her husband senses that his mother-in-law is quite put out and does not take kindly to Millie's profuse apologies. For the rest of the evening and well into the night, Millie bemoans how poor a daughter she is.*

> *To Sharon's consternation, Audrey has brought over a third "goodies basket."* I just can't get it out of my mind, Audrey says, how badly I treated you at the camp-out last weekend, and I just hope you'll accept this as a part of how much I owe you for my terrible behavior. *Sharon has already accepted two profuse apologies from Audrey and is at a loss to know what to say to her this time. Now, Sharon is beginning to feel guilty about becoming impatient with her friend.*

> Father, I know it's wrong to think like this, but I want to do something terrible to that man we had to find not

guilty. We were all sure that he was abusing his stepdaughter, but we agreed that the prosecution didn't prove it. *Father Paul is struggling to find a way to help his troubled parishoner, Al, work through both the obsession to right a wrong and the painful guilt that Al feels about having "evil" thoughts. For the thirty years that Father Paul has known Al, he has never seen Al do anything hurtful to anyone. Al is convinced that it is not "natural" for him to want the stepfather to suffer at his hands and feels that God will punish him severely for his "sinful ideas."*

To people for whom any preoccupation with personal guilt is unnecessary, silly, pathological, or all three, it may come as a surprise to learn that most of their acquaintances, close and distant, are still concerned about being responsible and do not easily dismiss the seriousness of harming others. Neither they nor any of their acquaintances may have anything to do with the rampant moral evil that threatens world stability today, but with everyone else they share in common at least minor offenses for which they are indeed guilty, whether they choose to acknowledge their guilt or not. From this perspective, the fact that some people tally even their imagined wrongdoings is no more odd than the fact that others keep no books at all on their real ones.

The spirituality of those who keep guilt feelings painfully before them is a spirituality dominated by overconscientiousness or perfectionism, by an obsessive preoccupation with the form of religion over its substance. Its relatively benign manifestation is the overvaluation of minor sins. Its more malignant one puts imagined sins on a par with real ones, to be fretted about as if they had been carried out rather than merely conjured about. An early sign of both preoccupations is a pattern of judging oneself harshly before others can express reactions of their own, for example:

I can't tell you how terribly, terribly sorry I am. I've messed up everything, haven't I? Nothing I do seems to come out right anymore, and it's a wonder that I keep on trying at all. Sometimes I just feel like giving up altogether.

I feel so alone right now that I can't even remember what the arguments with the kids were all about. I know I failed them in a lot of ways and that there's no getting back to what we had when they were real little. Maybe that's why I've been so sad for so long.

If I had paid more attention to the details, the whole event would have come off a lot better, and people wouldn't be so down about all the opportunities we missed. No wonder everybody's mad at me. They ought to just go ahead and fire me. I sure wouldn't have any grounds to complain.

Even the most sensitive and experienced caregivers can momentarily be rendered speechless by such outcries. There is so much to respond to that they may hardly know where to begin. In situations like these, it can be helpful to remind ourselves that indiscriminate self-blame and outpouring of misery can serve a manipulative purpose. The histrionics may be intended to cajole us into challenging the global self-criticism that the guilt-ridden person cannot challenge for himself or herself. Literally, we are being asked to talk him or her out of it, for example:

It hurts me to hear you put yourself down that way. You're a wonderful person, and I admire so much how hard you're trying to cope with a lot of bad things that have happened in your life. Sure you mess up once in a while, but who wouldn't, with all you've had to deal with?

Come on, it's not that bad. You did everything you could. Who has any right to ask more of you than what you've always tried to do for your kids? None of us is a perfect parent, you know.

Nobody is blaming you. A lot of the things you're blaming yourself for could have happened no matter how hard every-

> *body worked to make the thing a success. They're not your fault. Let's take another look at all you did do, so that you can give yourself a little credit, OK?*

Each of the caregivers who offered to their distraught care receivers the responses just quoted later shared with me a common assessment of how unhelpful their efforts proved to be. As one put it: *I knew I was getting sucked in, even as I heard myself trying to buck up my care receiver. And of course, what I said didn't work; all he did was tell me how little I understood about what he was really feeling. I came away from the conversation feeling really "had."* I asked this cherished friend how he now thinks he might have handled the situation differently. His reply was especially perceptive: *Actually, I did handle it differently, the very next time he and I talked. I asked my care receiver to shoot square with me about just how really torn up he was inside and to "fess up" that some of the things he keeps saying to me might have just a little attention-getting aim to them.*

What made this seemingly harsh comment effective was the level of trust that my friend had already established with his care receiver. Defensive, the care receiver first shot back, *What do you mean by that?* Not long after, however, he began to open up: *All this moaning and groaning must be nothing but irritating. I guess I beat up on myself so hard that sometimes I just need a little relief. Getting you to tell me I'm not so bad keeps the monkey off my back for a little while anyway. Geez, you must be getting sick of it.* (Long pause) *Uh-oh, there I go again!*

Two other aspects of the manipulation just described are worth noting. First, blaming oneself quickly and globally can divert attention away from genuine infractions against others and toward one's own self-centered needs and wants, which are now put forward as the proper subject of any further conversation:

> *I feel just awful about completely spoiling the party you worked so hard on. No doubt about it, my behavior was atrocious. I really do try to stay sober, but it's really, really hard for someone who grew up in the kind of family I grew up in to*

do it. My mom and dad drank all the time, you know, and I don't seem to be able to help myself any more than they could.

You just wouldn't believe the schedule I had yesterday, but I did it to myself. Like I've been doing more and more lately. It's just messing things up with all my friends. I just can't seem to get a handle on things, and I feel rotten about missing our lunch and lots of other things besides. Is our office ever going to get on top of it all?

Can you ever forgive me for the way I've been acting these past few weeks? I just haven't been myself. With ——— away all the time, and the kids demanding so much from me, and my mom needing more and more attention. It all seems more than I can handle.

The other aspect worth noting about someone's manipulating us to offer encouragement prematurely and excessively is that it serves to close off further dialogue about the wrongs that initiated the conversation in the first place. The momentary silence that the manipulative statements often generate confirms that the ploy has been effective. Taken aback, we may try so hard to make the other person feel better—and to feel better ourselves in the other's presence—that we fail to do the one thing most needed in the situation. We may fail to provide the challenge and encouragement that might help the other person take more responsibility for his or her own behavior. By way of examples, and with respect to the manipulative statements just quoted, instead of the rushing to reassure, we might respond with observations such as:

You're right: what you did at the party was pretty awful. And I want to accept your apology so that we can move on. But what's making it hard for me is that you're giving me a lot of reasons why what you did maybe wasn't your fault after all and that maybe you'll just have to keep on doing it in spite of yourself and me.

> *Right now I can't tell whether you're asking me to forgive you for something or whether you want me just to listen to how tough your schedule is these days. Could we take it one thing at a time?*
>
> *Sure I can forgive you, but it does bug me that I seem to be the one who's getting the brunt of a lot of your frustrations with other people in your life. Instead of just being so cross with me, how about letting me in on more of what's happening with you, and maybe together we can figure out what might make at least some things better.*

People who magnify the significance of relatively minor wrongs or who make little if any distinction between imagined and real offenses pose a unique challenge to those who care about them. On the one hand, they deserve the same kind of empathy, acceptance, and understanding that are the hallmarks of any caring relationship. On the other, they need to take more responsibility for their real wrongdoing and the guilt that properly accompanies it. Unhappily, even gentle prodding to reassess guilt realistically can be interpreted as confirmation of the guilt-ridden person's most egregious distortions of what he or she has and has not done to offend or harm someone else, for example: *You must be thinking how rotten I am, to be asking me what you just asked.*

These considerations lead us to the final concern of this section and chapter: the covering over of genuine guilt by clinging to unrealistic feelings of ineffectiveness and worthlessness. The most serious problem that holding on to unrealistic guilt poses for spiritual growth is that it can block us from dealing adequately with the guilt that we do have and for which we do need to make amends. There is a strange logic involved here. Though insisting that we are guilty, when we are not, can make us feel worse about ourselves than God feels about us, it also and paradoxically can create within us a sense of being righteous by virtue of the very guilt that we stubbornly refuse to let go. It is as if the humility exposed in being guilt-ridden will itself enhance our worth in God's eyes, even though the contrition we purport to feel rarely leads to genuine repentance, in the sense of a commitment to live our lives differently from here on.

At the heart of this oddly distorted spirituality is a pattern of flaying oneself for relatively minor infractions while studiously ignoring major ones. One pastor expressed it as "sweating a lot of little things so that we don't have to sweat the really big ones." By way of examples:

Samantha berates herself constantly for not giving more money to her church. Her pastor, however, knows that Samantha has been one of the parish's largest contributors for years. He is concerned instead about her refusal to talk at any length about repudiating, while a teenager, the church of her parents and believes that Samantha is feeling considerable guilt over the pain that her defection may have caused them.

Win confesses regularly to his priest, Father Denny, his concern about not being more faithful in his attendance at Mass, even though he is present for the early service at least five mornings a week and comes to most special services unless prevented by illness. From other parishioners, Father Denny has heard fragments of conversations about "people who do terrible things in their lives and still show their faces in church." He wonders whether Win might be one of the parishioners the others have in mind but is uncertain how he might proceed in finding out. His regular question to Win, *Is there anything else bothering you?* elicits the same answer each time: *No, Father, everything else is fine*.

Nora apologizes profusely to her fellow anti-abortion supporters for being out of the country during their most recent protest, and with trembling lips pledges that she will quit her job before she allows anything ever again to get in the way of participating in her church's "holy war" on abortion clinics. Nora's sister, Tammy, is beside herself with worry and uncertainty about whether Nora has ever talked with anyone about her own abortion during her teenage years. Taking Nora to a clinic for the abortion was the hardest thing that Tammy has ever had to do in her life.

Neither the distress that Samantha, Win, and Nora feel, nor the pain of its acknowledgment is in any way to be discounted.

These three faithful Christians need and fully deserve the kind of support they have sought, support that respects what they say, that affirms their worth in the sight of God and the church, and that expresses realistic hope that they will come to feel less driven and better about themselves all around. Nevertheless, the kind of encouragement in faith that Christian caring offers will also seek to help people struggling with the kind of unrealistic guilt that plagues these three care receivers to give thanks that they are open to acknowledging guilt at all and to ask God's help in discovering what their guilt and their guilt feelings are really about.

Summary

This chapter has explored two patterns of not dealing with guilt and guilt feelings responsibly: denial and excessive scrupulousness. Fundamental to the discussion of both is an insistence upon the accessibility of each to conscious reflection, deliberation, and change. This is not to dispute the claims of mental health professionals that these patterns often operate outside of our awareness and that it is sometimes difficult to break their hold on us. What the chapter does challenge is the notion that unconscious processes and patterns can wholly determine our actions and the ways we do and do not take responsibility for them. By God's grace, we know better.

CHAPTER FIVE

FORGIVENESS: GOD'S AND OURS

In general, guilt is healed through a process that involves forthright acknowledgment, apology, and amends-making by the wrongdoer, and good-faith acceptance of the efforts by the persons wronged. There are situations, however, in which wrongdoing, whether deliberate or inadvertent, unleashes consequences that are too painful for apologies to salve and too destructive for amends to compensate. The primary purpose of this chapter is to show how reconciliation is still possible in these extreme situations, but not by making amends. When harm is irreparable, amends cannot suffice. Only forgiveness can.

The Limits of Amends-Making

Even in ordinary life sitations, amends-making can falter. For example, the amends offered may be insufficient to compensate for the particular offense. For an expensive pen that she borrowed from Betty and lost, Sally offers as a substitute a knock-off version hastily purchased at a discount store. Or, the amends offered may carry adequate value, but still may be rejected for having been unilaterally determined by the offender. Jerry completes Dan's work on two clients' accounts in order to "pay him back" for failing to work overtime with him the previous weekend. Dan responds caustically by saying, *Well, sure, Jerry, I can use the help you gave, but what I was really hoping you'd do was interview the three guys we've been putting off for a week because we've been too busy to get back to them.*

A more significant breakdown of the amends-making process occurs when the offended party accepts the amends offered but resists or refuses—whether for good reasons or bad—restoration of the relationship itself. Donna notes with gratitude her boyfriend's apology for standing her up but chooses not to go out with him anymore. Two adult sisters are moved to tears by their father's apologies for abandoning them during their childhood but tell him bluntly that it is too late for there ever to be a relationship with him.

Donna and the sisters choose to move on from relationships damaged by others' wrongdoing because there is little likelihood of real change on the parts of those who hurt them. Though they deserve the amends offered them, they are under no obligation to become reconciled with their offenders merely because the offenders are seeking it and merely because they accept the amends offered. However, if the amends are accompanied by commitments to make the changes necessary to ensure that the offenses never occur again, and if these pledges are rejected, then the failure to achieve reconciliation may rest more with the offended parties than with the offending ones.

These examples bring out two especially important things about the amends-making process in everyday situations. The first is that either party to a relationship distressed by one member's offensive or harmful acts is free not to make the adjustments necessary to bring about reconciliation. The guilty party can refuse to make clearly warranted amends, and the injured party can either refuse to accept amends offered at all, or accept them as compensation deserved, while giving up on the relationship itself. Second, for people genuinely committed to bringing about reconciliation in damaged relationships, there is a clear, step-by-step process for accomplishing the task.

Unhappily, however, not all situations marked by wrongdoing are everyday in character. Some are of the sort illustrated at the end of chapter 3 in the narrative of Hal's inadvertent running over of a child with his car. Clearly, here is a situation in which ordinary ways of dealing with one person's bringing harm to another person cannot help. There are many other situations like this, all created by a panoply of thoughtless, careless, and sometimes intentionally destructive acts that no human being should inflict upon anyone under any circumstances, for example:

George is facing criminal charges for embezzlement, stemming from a false accusation by a former partner, who is seeking to cut a deal with the prosecution.

Wanda and Bill are still grief-stricken two years after an incompetent surgeon botched minor surgery on their three-year-old daughter, resulting in her altogether unnecessary death.

Tom, carefully maintaining the speed limit while driving through a wealthy suburb in midevening, is pulled over by a white policeman who is wondering why any black man should be in the neighborhood at all.

Thousands of families may never be able to resume lives shattered by terrorists in hijacked airplanes.

This last case illustrates especially vividly the extreme situations with which people around the world constantly struggle. Families and whole communities must grapple all too often with both negligent and terrorist acts that inflict undeserved pain, grief, despair, and death on truly innocent people. In such situations, God's call to become agents of peace may be countered by a lust for vengeance that can put reconciliation between people, and between humanity and God, permanently out of reach.

It is not only terrorist acts, however, that bring us face-to-face with the problem of irreparable harm and unsatisfiable guilt. Inadvertent acts of basically good people do also. In the horrifying situation that holds Hal and the parents of a dead child in what could become a spiritual death grip, one of life's most profound and difficult questions becomes inescapable: When our actions, whether mistaken or malicious, bring about consequences whose destructiveness is beyond repair, what can we do to bring about reconciliation with those we harm? What can a businessman, who leaves his partner's reputation in shambles, possibly do to make up for the diminished future of his falsely accused victim? What can a physician, whose ill preparedness and arrogance claim an innocent girl's life, possibly do to compensate her grieving parents for a sadness that knows no surcease? What can a white police officer, having now given his community's racist attitudes fresh expression, possibly do to overcome the years of anguish that one man has already endured on streets from which others would bar him? What can hate-filled people possibly do to transform their contemptuousness into respectfulness, their tearing down into building up, their despair into hope, and those they would destroy into those they would serve?

To questions like these, our faith tradition offers a two-part answer. First, because some of our transgressions—whether against ourselves, others, or God—are beyond our capacity to atone for, their destructive consequences can be overcome only when the injured themselves initiate the one action that alone can help: forgiveness. And second, victimizers must both desire reconciliation and accept the forgiveness that makes reconciliation possible. In Hal's case, only if the parents of the dead child can find it in their hearts not to blame him for what happened, and only if Hal can get beyond blaming himself, can restoration of their relationship come about. Similarly, only if George, Wanda, Bill, Tom, and victims of terrorism everywhere choose no longer to hold against their persecutors what has been done to them can reconciliation occur. Even then, their persecutors must decide that they want reconciliation to occur and that they will throw themselves on the mercy of the very persons they seek to harm.

What Forgiveness Is Not

The kind of forgiveness just described can be misunderstood in several different ways. For some people, to forgive means to pretend that something offensive or harmful did not occur at all, for example: *Let's just agree that this never happened, and get on with our lives*. For others, to forgive means to forget, for example: *What's done is done, and we can't change that fact. So just put it out of your mind completely. That's what I'm going to do*. From the standpoint of both perspectives, even the faintest residue of memory about the original transgression can only compromise the reconciliation process and tangle the relationship in unfinished agendas:

> *I hear you when you say you're still feeling bad about what you did, but I really don't want to talk about it. Why keep dwelling on something that we've already let go of? It doesn't exist any more! Can't you get that?*
>
> *So we're back to that again. When are we going to get this behind us?*
>
> *You've forgiven me; I know that. What's wrong with me that I can't seem to forgive myself? I've gotta push this completely out of my mind because things won't be right between us until I do.*

To an extent, all of these responses may be appropriate to their respective situations. If forgiveness proceeds from the commitment of a wronged person no longer to count the wrong against the wrongdoer, then it is indeed out of line for the one forgiven to keep bringing up painful reminders of the initial wrong, to dwell on the wrong incessantly, or to challenge the victim's decision to forgive in the first place. Forgiveness, however, cannot be genuine if it is part of a collusion to deny or forget real wrongs.

It is precisely its attentiveness to and respect for reality that make forgiveness the powerful means to reconciliation that it is. At their most authentic, acts of forgiveness reflect a complex process that begins not with denying and forgetting, but rather with facing offenses, hurts, harm, and evil squarely and acknowledging them fully, along with the claims they make on wrongdoers to rectify their wrongdoing. The process continues by affirming every victimized person's right to restitution. Finally, on the basis of responsible deliberation rather than emotions of the moment, it comes to completion in a conscious decision—in contrast with an emotional reaction of the moment—to suspend the demands of justice for the sake of restoring a relationship.

There are other ways to misunderstand what forgiveness is besides confusing it with treating a wrong as if it never happened or with refusing to recall it. One way, mentioned briefly earlier in this chapter, assumes that offenses can be forgiven as long as those who commit them confess honestly what they have done, express sorrow about it, and pledge earnestly never to do it again. On the face of it, this way of looking at the matter is sensible. Offering forgiveness to people who are neither sorry for their wrongdoing nor willing to stop it can weaken the moral fabric of relationships and communities to such an extent that some of the most basic elements of human decency and civility—such as obligation, responsibility, and justice—are rendered superfluous.

When applied to the everyday kinds of offense and hurt we inflict on people, the insistence that forgiveness follow upon repentance is eminently practical. Most of the wrongs we do that fall into this category can be dealt with readily, to the betterment of our relationships, when we allow ourselves to feel the constraint placed upon us by another's demand for acknowledgment and apology, even if not for amends. However, applying this practical principle to the more extreme situations created by our mistakes, thoughtlessness, self-centeredness, and willful destructiveness is more problematic.

In the first place, as we have seen, some harm outweighs anything that acknowledgments, apologies, and amends-making can possibly accomplish. Second, making repentance a condition of forgiveness flies in the face of the Christian faith's foundational understanding of God's loving us unconditionally and calling us to love others in this same spirit. Certainly, many New Testament texts speak of turning to God in contrition and hoping for a positive response on God's part as a result. However, the message of the New Testament as a whole on this subject is utterly clear: In Jesus Christ, God conveys forgiveness of our sins as a sheer act of grace. Rather than a condition for God's forgiving us, repentance is a grateful response to forgiveness already rendered.

Just as some people see contrition and repentance as conditions that must be fulfilled before forgiveness can even be considered, others believe that not even the most abject contrition and repentance can warrant forgiveness for some acts at all. In explicitly Christian terms, there are both forgivable and unforgivable sins. This misunderstanding of forgiveness is especially complex as well as vexing, so much so that it warrants a fuller exploration than can be given in a paragraph or two. Accordingly, the whole of the next section will be devoted to it.

About the Unforgivable Sin

Most people share a common revulsion toward perfidious acts such as sexual assault, torture, or murder, and if there really are unforgivable offenses, these would surely fit the category. Over the course of my ministry, however, I have repeatedly encountered total denunciations of acts that fall far short of constituting irredeemable moral turpitude, such as adultery, doubt, divorce, remarriage after divorce, homosexuality, unorthodox beliefs, abortion, disrespect of parents, violating the first commandment—to name just a few. Some people I know who are guilty of one or more of these behaviors live in terror of being punished everlastingly for their transgressions. Other people I know, who are guilty of none of them, bask contentedly in absolute certainty about the fate of people who are guilty. The certitude that usually accompanies both guilt about and denunciations of such behaviors and attitudes tends to be as unshakeable as it is awesome. And yet, serious questions can and should be raised about branding anyone who may be guilty of them, including ourselves, as beyond redemption.

The most obvious question is whether everything on this second list is an example of wrongdoing at all. We may have little doubt about the wrongness of adultery or of loving God with less than our whole being. We have fewer grounds for certainty about the other behaviors and attitudes cited, at least if our certainty extends to condemning these things as totally wrong under all circumstances. This brings us to a second question: Even if all of these items are indeed examples of wrongdoing, do circumstances have any role to play in our assessment of the *degree* of their wrongfulness?

If it is unacceptable, for example, to be doubtful or to hold unorthodox beliefs, is every form of doubting and of unorthodox belief equally repellent, or are some forms more blameworthy than others? Is every divorce as reprehensible as every other divorce? Is the remarriage of a woman who divorced her first husband after years of being abused by him as out of line as the remarriage of a man who impulsively left his wife and children for a younger, more attractive, and wealthier woman? Is homosexual activity in a committed relationship as deserving of condemnation as promiscuous homosexual behavior in a series of one-night stands? Is the abortion of a fetus irreparably damaged from a genetic anomaly as wrong as the abortion of a fetus by parents who have determined that the children they already have are enough? Is the disrespect shown a father by the daughter he assaulted throughout childhood no worse than the disrespect shown a mother by her petulant, self-absorbed, overindulged adolescent daughter?

A major problem with the very notion of unforgivable offenses is that it makes impossible even exploring, much less answering, questions like these. Does this mean that we have no grounds at all for considering the possibility that some wrongdoing may be beyond forgiving? From the standpoint of our faith tradition, we would be on shaky terrain were we to say so. Because there is clear mention in several New Testament books of unpardonable guilt—such as in Hebrews, 1 John—we cannot dismiss out of hand the strong conviction held by many about absolute limits on forgiveness, even if the conviction is often applied too broadly and its applications defended less than adequately.

The most explicit statement in the New Testament about wrongdoing beyond the realm of grace and forgiveness is found in Mark 3:28-29. There, Jesus is quoted as follows: *Truly I tell you: every sin and every slander can be forgiven; but whoever slanders the Holy Spirit can never be forgiven; he is guilty of an eternal sin* (REB). The context for Jesus' startling statement is an accusation that he can exorcise demons because he is in league with Satan. In reply, Jesus first points out the strange contradiction borne by this allegation—Satan is at odds with his own demonic emissaries—and then, as Mark implies, goes on to attribute the real power behind his exorcisms to God, who is not to be slandered or, in the King James rendering, "blasphemed," upon pain of eternal damnation.

Jesus' words about an offense that forever separates perpetrators from God reoccur in Luke 12:10, but in a context different from the one described by Mark. That Luke is so careful to preserve the teaching at all, even though it conflicts with the very strong emphasis on forgiveness that runs through his Gospel, indicates just how firmly set in early Christian belief these words must have been. Matthew's treatment of the teaching preserves Mark's setting, but Jesus' words themselves are expanded somewhat (as they are also in Luke): *Anyone who speaks a word against the Son of Man will be forgiven; but if anyone speaks against the Holy Spirit, for him there will be no forgiveness, either in this age or in the age to come* (12:32 REB). Here, Jesus is concerned to make unmistakably clear that the issue is not slander heaped upon him, but rather slander directed against the power of God that is in him. Interestingly, Paul seems to disagree: *No one who says "A curse on Jesus!" can be speaking under the influence of the Spirit of God; and no one can say "Jesus is Lord!" except under the influence of the Holy Spirit* (1 Cor. 12:3 REB).

Mark, Matthew, and Luke all suggest that what makes an act unforgivable is more the contempt it shows toward God than the damage it inflicts on human relationships. God is the primary offended party; the refusal to forgive is God's choice, not human beings'; and the consequences of God's refusal are eternal as well as temporal. What this means for our own relationships is that we do not have a right to regard another's offense against us, no matter what it may be, as unforgivable in principle. Withholding forgiveness is a divine prerogative exclusively.

Other New Testament passages look at the matter a little differently. First John, preoccupied with the numbers of former believers who have "left our ranks," refers at its close to a "deadly sin" beyond the power of others' intercession and the willingness of God to heal (5:16). What the writer seems to have in mind is the sin of secession, or apostasy: once faithful members of the Johannine community are so no longer. John has no doubt that their leaving is offensive to God. His more urgent concern, however, is with the devastating effect of their departure on the community they leave behind. Hebrews conceives unforgivable sin in much this same way. It is a "falling away" from God, but even more from a mode of living once shared with others in the Holy Spirit (6:4-6). These two passages are quite emphatic about the effect of "deadly sin" on our relationships with one another as well as with God. Nevertheless, they also share in common with the texts previously discussed from the Gospels the conviction that what makes wrongdoing unforgivable is God's judgment and not ours.

Together, all of the New Testament passages cited above share the view that whatever we may believe unforgivable sin to be, that sin is singular and not plural in nature. Whether it is attributing to Satan the power that is God's alone or abandoning the shared life of a community of faith or rejecting rather than praising Jesus, the sin that separates us from God forever is one kind of sin only, not many kinds. In Mark's rendering, upon which the Christian tradition has depended more than on any other, the one and only thing that God will never forgive is slandering the animating power of Jesus' ministry. About this definition, we can draw two important conclusions immediately. One is that many people who are worried about committing the unpardonable offense have neither committed it nor are likely ever to commit it. The second is that those who delight in searching out the many ways others follow to perdition should ease off from their labors; there is only one compromising act for which they can hold us accountable. Every other kind of wrongdoing, against self, others, and God, can be forgiven. The truly startling character of this affirmation is perhaps best appreciated by applying it to the offenses referred to in the first sentence of this section.

There is a serious pastoral issue involved in the process of uncovering what the New Testament does and does not teach about redeemable and irredeemable sin. It is this: Fretting about the possibility of committing an unforgivable sin is inimical to living a grace-filled life. In the first place, it is not at all clear that Jesus' condemning words about slandering the Holy Spirit were meant to apply to situations beyond that which provoked them in the first place. Struggling to minister to the rapidly growing crowds following him excitedly from one Galilean town to another, Jesus is interrupted constantly by condescending scribes "down from Jerusalem." Adroitly maneuvering to identify Jesus with the demon possessed, the scribes all of a sudden find themselves caught in a rhetorical trap of their own devising: The very suggestion that Jesus' exorcisms are demon inspired becomes the primary evidence for attributing Satanic influence to the accusers themselves. Matthew situates Jesus' teaching in the same way that Mark does, but he substitutes the Pharisees for the scribes as its recipients. Only Luke removes Jesus' words from this specific polemical context and places them alongside several other sayings uttered to "a crowd of many thousands" (Luke 12:1 REB). However, that the collection of sayings is prefaced by Jesus' warning to be on guard against the Pharisees strongly suggests that Luke may simply have presupposed the original setting of the words about unforgivable sin, without reproducing its details explicitly.

There is a second pastoral reason for questioning just how much we can generalize from Jesus' teaching about an unforgivable sin. It derives from subsequent Christian tradition, specifically from words familiar to us in the Apostles' Creed: *I believe in the forgiveness of sins*. Though the creed itself emerged from the Christian community in Rome during the latter half of the second century, its affirmations mirror those of the apostolic age. What is especially striking about the article just quoted from it is its unambiguous expression of God's limitless grace: All sins, not some or most, are enveloped in God's love. It suggests that the concerns of first-century Christians about sins beyond the possibility of redemption were soon swallowed up in praise for the all-surpassing power of God to overcome any and every obstacle to fellowship with him. Nothing in all creation—not even our most grievous sins—can, in Paul's words, finally separate us from the love of God in Christ Jesus our Lord (Rom. 8:39).

To affirm that we are forgiven sinners is not to minimize the seriousness of the sins themselves, or the effort on God's part both to redeem us from them and to communicate God's redemption to us. Human sinfulness is panoramic in scope, encompassing an astonishing range of both less and more serious sins alike—in Roman Catholic terms, "venial" and "mortal" sins, respectively. Together, all our sins rightly demand from us some combination of inward acknowledgment, outward confession, contrition, repentance, and penance. Even the most heinous sin, however, does not by the mere act of committing it damn the wrongdoer eternally. God's love will remain steadfast, in spite of the alienation we bring about by our wrongdoing.

Forgiveness Without Reconciliation

The final misunderstanding of forgiveness to be identified in this chapter is one mentioned earlier in another context. It rests upon confusing a decision to forgive people with a willingness to become reconciled with them. By way of example, Ellen is reeling from a negative performance review by a supervisor who misplaced, and then forgot about, data that showed her work to be exemplary in several different areas. Though the supervisor has since apologized, and though Ellen is disposed to forgive the mistakes and move on, she hesitates. A trusted friend, with whom Ellen has been talking about the matter, gently asks: *But something's holding you back, isn't it? What do you think it could be?* Ellen responds: *I know it sounds crazy, but I just don't want to be around that man anymore, and if I forgive this then there's nothing for me to do but to keep on working for him.* Her friend helpfully reminds Ellen that she actually has at least three other options available, and not just one: *There's no reason to stay stuck like this. You don't have to be forgiving at all; stay at your desk and stay mad, too. Or forgive him, but still move on. And of course, you could move on and not forgive him at all.*

Of the three options wisely offered Ellen by her caring friend, the second is especially important to the present discussion. It illustrates well a profoundly important spiritual truth: Though forgiveness makes reconciliation possible, it does not make reconciliation mandatory. We can forgive someone's offensive and hurtful actions toward us, in the sense that we choose not to demand amends for them, and at the same time we can exercise our right not to continue the relationship in which the actions occurred. We can exercise this right even if the other person exhibits both a desire and a willingness to make whatever changes we might ask, for the sake of putting the relationship on a new footing. Because forgiveness is an undeserved gift, we always have the right to withhold offering it, and those whom we offend have the right to withhold it from us. Just as forgiveness itself is a gift, so is the reconciliation that forgiveness makes possible. We can choose not to forgive, *and* we can choose not to become reconciled with those we do forgive.

For some people, it is only in separating the act of forgiveness from maintaining a relationship that forgiveness becomes possible at all, for example:

- for a high-school honors student whose math teacher, after falsely accusing him of cheating on an exam, failed him for the course;

- for an Arab family whose small grocery store lies in ruins following an attack by American neighbors loudly chanting "Terrorists go home!";
- for a young woman whose father, the perpetrator of incest throughout her early adolescent years, pressures to "walk her down the aisle" on her wedding day;
- for a respected African American member of a suburban community whose all-white country club turned down his application for membership;
- for an elderly man beaten nearly to death by his forty-year-old son during a furious search of their house for money to buy drugs.

The respective victims in all of these (actual) cases responded to their situations in the same way: All chose to forgive their victimizers *and* to maintain as much distance between themselves and those who harmed them as their circumstances permitted. The African American man referred to above had especially eloquent words to say about how he coped with his own situation:

> *A lot of my friends kept reminding me that we all had a stake in this and that I owed it to everybody to keep the pressure on that club. But I finally realized that neither I nor my friends were going to find any real friendships in that place, at least for an awfully long time, and that just as I had the right to keep on championing a cause, I also had the right not to pursue relationships that didn't look good to me. And you know what? I didn't feel angry at those members anymore or that they owed me anything. Liberating! Although a different kind of liberation than I was after at first.*

What, Then, *Is* Forgiveness?

We have been looking at misunderstandings of what forgiveness is, or, to put it another way, at what forgiveness is not. Whatever forgiveness is, it is not: treating an offense as if it never happened; forgetting that it actually did happen; absolving a transgressor only upon his or her prior repentance for the wrong done; distinguishing forgivable sins from unforgivable ones and withholding forgiveness of the latter; or fulfilling a sense of obligation to reconcile even with those who wrong us repeatedly. What forgiveness *is* is the subject of the final section of the chapter.

One of the most important statements about forgiveness in all of the Bible is embedded in the passage quoted earlier in this book from Paul: *God was in Christ reconciling the world to himself, no longer holding people's misdeeds against them* (2 Cor. 5:19 REB). What Paul here calls "misdeeds" can be understood as offensive or harmful acts for which their perpetrators are obliged to atone. People wronged by them—other people and God—have the right to count the transgressions and their destructive consequences against those who commit them and to hold on to their claims for justice until the claims are satisfied. Whether in response to amends completed or to a mutual recognition that amends are not possible, forgiveness is the decision of a wronged party to relinquish his or her legitimate claim to satisfaction and to dwell no longer on whatever distress the initial transgression caused.

Forgiveness can be the first step toward (a) restoring a relationship to its condition prior to the wrongdoing that now jeopardizes it; (b) leaving a hurtful relationship behind altogether; or (c) drawing both wounder and wounded into a new relationship marked by deeper understanding and compassion. About (a), our faith is unambiguous: God calls us to seek peace in every relationship. As Paul wrote to the Philippians, *Let your bearing towards one another arise out of your life in Christ Jesus* (2:5 NEB). That we are obligated to remain open to restoration in relationships marked by alienation does not imply, however, that we are the only parties to the relationship who bear responsibility for its wholeness. No matter how clearly and earnestly we communicate a desire for and a commitment to reconciliation, some who offend us, and some whom we offend, may be unwilling to join us in an effort to repair the damages they or we do to the respective relationships. The same God-given freedom to offer forgiveness to one other is also the freedom not to forgive at all, not to accept forgiveness when it is offered, and not to reenter the relationship that wrongdoing may have torn apart.

About (b) above—forgiving someone but refusing to stay in a relationship with him or her—if our faith cannot support us wholly in our decision, it can and does offer us strong consolation when circumstances require us to make it. Why only limited support? Because human beings are created for partnership with God in caring for the created order, together. Alienated relationships run counter to fulfilling our divinely bestowed destiny and to experiencing the joy that God intends for all humanity in a universal, divinely sustained human fellowship. Even though we may be at odds with someone through no fault of our own, the knowledge that the alienation is not God's desire for either of us can still be very painful. What helps is the faith that we are not alone in longing for an end to the hostility. When all of our best efforts toward bringing about reconciliation fail, we can at least take consolation from trusting that God grieves as much as we do.

The consolation that faith offers us includes the soothing comfort that the word itself would lead us to expect. More important, however, the consolation of faith is the strengthening presence of the Holy Spirit, assuring us that we are not alone, that God is with us, and that healthy relationships await us on the far side of unhealthy ones. Though God at all times and everywhere continues God's work of reconciling the world to himself, not all human relationships are reconcilable at every moment of their own history. Leaving relationships that are not now reconcilable for the sake of those that are can be reasonable, moral, and just, even as we struggle with the resulting loneliness and the residue of frustration and even bitterness. In the struggle, it can be powerfully consoling to keep in view faith's vision of God the Reconciler, never resting content until the last iota of enmity in the created order is finally overcome and transformed by his all-sufficient love.

If forgiveness—offered and received—can be the first step toward restoring one relationship and toward leaving another behind, it can also and more importantly raise still other relationships to a new and higher level of mutual respect, faithfulness, and gratitude. By not holding a wrong done to us against the one who commits it, our relationship with that person can escape the contamination that outrage, resentment, and guilt might inflict upon it. By abrogating claims to recompense for being wronged, even and especially claims that are just by any reasonable standard, we can break the power of wrongdoing to determine by itself the future of relationships that the wrongdoing otherwise threatens. A decision to be forgiving, especially when we have good reasons for withholding it, or a decision to accept forgiveness, especially when we know we do not deserve it, is a decision for grace over law, love over justice, the future over the past, and above all, for committing ourselves to God's plan for the human community as a whole over clinging obstinately to our own false sense of entitlement or unworthiness.

As we have seen, not every relationship lends itself to such decisions. Sometimes, only restoration is possible, not growth. Other times, only the ending of one relationship can make possible a healthier relationship with someone else. But among people for whom reconciliation is the fruit of forgiveness lovingly offered and graciously received, God dwells with an especially joyful heart.

Summary

Most relationships infected by wrongdoing can be restored to good health through a process of acknowledgment, apology, and amends-making. "Most" is the key word here, for not all alienated relationships are reconcilable by these means. This chapter has focused on relationships devastated by offensive, hurtful, and destructive behaviors beyond the capacity of their perpetrators to atone for, and on the once source of hope for them, forgiveness. Just as God forgives our own "trespasses," we are to forgive those who trespass against us. How we can become more forgiving people ourselves, in gratitude for what God has done for us, and how we can help others become more forgiving in their own lives, are the principal issues to be dealt with in the next two chapters.

CHAPTER SIX

MUST WE FORGIVE, AFTER ALL?

At the very heart of our faith is the call to forgive ourselves and others as God forgives us. Heeding God's call is more than merely a way beyond guilt, bitterness, self-protectiveness, and estrangement in relationships. It is *the* way—the best and sometimes only way. Why it is so difficult to follow in this way, and how we can overcome our resistance to doing so, are the primary concerns of this chapter.

Forgiveness, or Just Cheap Grace?

There is a profound spiritual dilemma posed by God's call to forgive, one that is not easy to resolve. It arises from the fact that "turning the other cheek" to mistreatment, as God desires, puts people—ourselves included—at risk for still further injustices and exploitation. Today as always, the truly innocent suffer all kinds of insensitive, offensive, degrading, and destructive acts from other people. They rightly cry out in anguish and protest, asking redress from the perpetrators and support from the rest of us. Does not encouraging them simply to forgive their abusers fail them in their time of greatest need? Is God not calling us to stand in solidarity with the truly victimized in their fearful, angry, and sometimes despairing protests against the evils of this world? And yet, if God is calling all of humanity to become a truly reconciled people, we cannot heed that call as long as we are filled with guilt and anger over our own and others' wrongdoing and put the rectifying of personal slights and offenses above building lasting, trustworthy relationships.

From a psychological perspective, withholding forgiveness makes us increasingly vulnerable to bitterness and hostility, to thinking only the worst of others, and to alienation from our own best self. Mental health professionals consistently remind us that however much we may want to believe that some combination of retaliation and redress will give us lasting relief from the suffering that others' transgressions cause us, we are still better off putting our grievances behind us. Why? Because holding on to them makes our sense of personal well-being too dependent on whether or not the person who hurt us owns up to his or her actions and does something to make things better between us. In the final analysis, we should forgive others because it is in our own best interest to do so, whether reconciliation comes from it or not.

There is considerable wisdom in this point of view. Enlightened balancing of self-interest with what our relationships require of us is an important part of becoming emotionally and spiritually mature. There is one relationship, however, that psychology does not bring adequately into view: our relationship with God and our divinely revealed obligation to forgive those who wrong us, even when being forgiving puts us at greater rather than lesser risk. Luke's Gospel offers us an especially powerful image of what that obligation looks like when it is lived out before others: Jesus' poignant petition to God to forgive his persecutors, uttered as he hung on a cross (Luke 23:34). In addition, then, to all the other negative consequences for our emotional and mental health of resisting being forgiving, there is one that only faith can fully understand: a growing estrangement from our Creator.

In the light of these considerations, how then can we depend upon forgiveness to promote peace in the world without weakening sensitivity to the magnitude of human suffering, that everywhere is crying out for alleviation? How can we balance our call to forgive from a loving spirit with our responsibility to pursue justice for all of God's creatures? The remaining sections of this chapter show how we can confront this spiritual dilemma honestly and experience anew the way through it that God has opened to us in Jesus Christ.

Jesus on Forgiveness: The Texts

In Matthew's Gospel, there is an interesting interchange between Jesus and Peter shortly after Peter's elevation to a place of special prominence among the disciples. The subject of the interchange is forgiveness, and it is introduced by a question that Peter brings to Jesus: *Lord, how often must I forgive my brother if he wrongs me?* (Matt. 18:21 JB). Peter then offers for Jesus' consideration his own working answer to the question: seven times. Jesus' reply is eye opening: not seven times, but seventy times seven.

Luke presents Jesus' teaching somewhat differently. First, the teaching is included as one of several things Jesus says, not to Peter in particular, and not in response to a question, but to all the disciples together on his own initiative. Second, the details of the teaching vary from Matthew's version: *If your brother does wrong, reprove him; and if he repents, forgive him. Even if he wrongs you seven times in a day and comes back to you seven times saying, "I am sorry," you are to forgive him* (Luke 17:3-4 REB). That Matthew and Luke place this particular conversation in different settings is of no real consequence for our understanding of the teaching it contains. Other differences, however, warrant closer examination. To that end, it may be helpful to set the two accounts alongside an Old Testament text that seems to serve as common background for both.

In one of the Bible's earliest passages, a genealogy traces descendants of Cain to a truly forbidding figure, Lamech, whom ancient Israel remembered for his pledge of swift and terrible revenge on any man who wounds him. He threatened a seventy-sevenfold retaliation, deliberately in contrast with the sevenfold retaliation that God earlier promised for the far greater offense of killing Cain (Gen. 4:15, 19-24). Two things about this story capture attention. One is the horrific intensity of Lamech's lust for revenge. The other is the awesome scope of Lamech's blasphemy. Without a thought, he takes it upon himself to redefine God's own criterion for responding to wrongdoing.

Though unnerving for their readers to contemplate, the picture that Luke and Matthew give of Jesus in the passages quoted above is the picture of a man who bears more than passing resemblance to Lamech. In particular, like Lamech, Jesus asserts in no uncertain terms his authoritativeness over a received tradition believed to originate from God. From here on, however, to our relief, the differences between the two swallow up the similarities. The fundamental difference is that while Lamech's posturing is for the sake of self-aggrandizement only, Jesus' bold act of standing a revered text from the Torah on its head is for the sake of bearing witness to a deeper truth about God. In Jesus' unfolding of this deeper truth, a criterion once proposed for exacting vengeance becomes in a blink of an eye a criterion for bestowing on people the very opposite of vengeance.

The way that Jesus speaks to Peter (in Matthew) or to the disciples as a whole (in Luke) about forgiveness shows that Jesus' closest companions already share at least a partial grasp of his fundamental principle, that vengeance must be replaced by forgiveness. All appear to agree that the idea of God's exacting vengeance seven times can and should be recast into a divine command to forgive seven times, but only seven times. What they do not grasp is that forgiveness has no limits at all. In pressing Jesus to be more specific about the number of times we are obliged to forgive, Peter comes close to deforming good news about a forgiving God into yet another law, this time one that sets out parameters for bestowing forgiveness without any more strain than necessary.

Jesus' response to the question about how many times we must forgive transcends conjuring with rules altogether, as well as the number crunching that all too often goes with it. In Luke's version of the response, Jesus works only with the number seven but presses it well beyond its original application in Genesis 4:15. Instead of limiting forgiveness to seven times an offense, Jesus insists that we are obliged to forgive wrongdoing seven times a day. Do these words amount to mere linear addition, making a new law only a little more difficult, but not impossible, to fulfill? Hardly, as Matthew's version of the same response makes clear. Here, Jesus picks up on Lamech's extension of a sevenfold response to a seventy-sevenfold one and then deliberately multiplies the extension beyond all reasonable limits. Now, we are asked to forgive not just up to seven times for every offense, or up to seven times a day indefinitely, but up to seventy times seven times.

Of course, this way of putting the matter—if taken at face value—still leaves open to Peter and to all who think like he did here the possibility of trying to make peace somehow with the much larger number and of taking comfort from knowing that there is still a finite end to our having to forgive someone. But if the absurdity of construing Jesus' teaching this way is not clear on the very face of it, the larger context within which Matthew in particular situates the teaching surely will make it so. Immediately following his counseling Peter to forgive wrongdoers 490 times, Jesus introduces a parable whose central meaning is unmistakable. A king's servant who owes his sovereign "ten thousand talents" begs for more time to repay the debt and receives, instead, his king's cancellation of the debt in its entirety. Rather than emulate the king's graciousness, however, the servant promptly goes out and demands repayment of a "hundred denarii" debt owed him by a fellow servant. After hearing of this outrage, the king sends for the servant who betrayed his generosity and orders him tortured until the original debt is paid in full. Jesus concludes the story by saying that unless we forgive others, God will treat us the way this king finally treated his unforgiving servant (Matt. 18:23-35).

Strictly speaking, this parable does not fit the particular teaching with which Matthew connects it. In specific, there is nothing in Jesus' story about our having to forgive people repeatedly. What the story does contain, however, through its numerical references to money owed, is a breathtaking view of the magnitude of forgiveness itself. In Jesus' day, the one hundred denarii that one servant in the story owes a fellow servant is roughly the wage earned by one hundred days of work. The ten thousand talents owed to the king is an almost incalculably larger figure, a rough equivalent of fifty million denarii or more. By framing the story in such exaggerated terms—the numbers utterly overwhelm literalism in the reading of the parable—Jesus clearly intends to communicate that God's forgiveness, unlike ours, is limitless and inexhaustible. Just as the scope of our indebtedness to God, because of our manifold wrongdoing, is beyond imagining, the graciousness of God's not counting that indebtedness against us is beyond understanding. How can we possibly repay God's incomprehensible mercifulness toward us? By being merciful to those who wrong us. We are, Jesus suggests, like the king's servant who is owed one hundred days' wages. This is a significant "account receivable," and forgiving it will not be easy for most of us. We are quite able, however, to do it. God requires that we do it *because* he has forgiven us so much more.

Jesus' central teaching about forgiveness, then, tightly binds God's forgiving us with our forgiving others. This theme is especially prominent in the Lord's Prayer: *Forgive us our debts, as we also have forgiven our debtors* (Matt. 6:12 NIV). As has been discussed in earlier chapters of this book, the harm that our actions bring upon others puts us in a state of indebtedness, which either we must remedy or the persons we harm must annul, if there is to be reconciliation between us. Though important parts of the process, therefore, being forgiven for and correcting our offensive and hurtful behaviors are not enough. The obligations we incur by virtue of the behaviors demand satisfaction in their own right, independently of what we do to change our ways for the future of our relationships.

In this light, what Jesus asks is that when we are wronged, we bring about the requisite satisfaction ourselves, by forgiving rather than demanding payment of what others owe us. As Paul reminds us, Jesus himself gave the supreme example of such forgiveness, by taking the satisfaction of all humankind's wrongdoing upon himself: *Christ died for us while we were yet sinners, and that is God's own proof of his love towards us* (Rom. 5:8 REB). Thus, the writer of the letter to the church at Ephesus, whether Paul or one of his followers, can enjoin his fellow believers: *Be friends with one another, and kind, forgiving each other as readily as God forgave you in Christ* (Eph. 4:32 JB).

Immediately after setting before his readers the Lord's Prayer itself, Matthew appends a statement from Jesus that puts his teaching about forgiveness in the strongest possible language: *Yes, if you forgive others their failings, your heavenly Father will forgive you yours; but if you do not forgive others, your Father will not forgive your failings either* (Matt. 6:14-15 JB). In the same translation, Mark's version of the statement reads: *And when you stand in prayer, forgive whatever you have against anybody, so that your Father in heaven may forgive your failings too* (Mark 11:25 JB). Along with the conclusion to the parable of the unforgiving servant, these words suggest that though God's gift of forgiveness is limitless, it comes with a condition attached. No matter how we translate the reference in the Lord's Prayer to our forgiving others—namely, as having forgiven them already, before we ask for God's forgiveness (Matthew: REB, JB, NSRV, NIV), or as forgiving them in the moment of our asking God to forgive us (Matthew: KJV, TEV; Luke: all translations)—God's forgiveness is inextricably linked with ours. As God forgives us, we must forgive others.

As clear as these words are, they can and do lead to seriously flawed applications when they are wrenched from the context of

Jesus' message as a whole. The major misapplication results from focusing too narrowly upon the forgive-or-else quality of Matthew's wording. A brief vignette will illustrate what can happen when we take his rendering too literally.

Nora is struggling to pay off debts incurred after her insurance company refused to pay for an experimental treatment that saved her youngest child's life. Though grateful for the monetary help she received from family members and friends, Nora is bitter about her plight and sees no way of ever regaining financial stability. Now plagued by persisting illnesses herself, she is convinced that her failing health is due to her inability to forgive those in the insurance company who denied her original claims. To her pastor, Patsy, Nora says tremblingly, *Patsy, God's going to make things even worse for me if I don't stop blaming those people, but I just can't seem to let go of it. I'm being a terrible Christian. I just keep on wishing the worst for them even though I know I shouldn't.* The conversation continues:

Patsy: The debts just won't go away, you keep on getting sick, you're scared about God's reaction to your being so angry—it's just an awful place to be in right now.

Nora: Not just right now, Patsy. I've been in this place for a long time.

P: And you're thinking that it isn't going to get any better.

N: I don't deserve for things to get better.

P: Because you won't forgive?

N: My Bible says that if I don't forgive, God won't forgive me.

P: And that God will also punish you by keeping you sick and in debt?

N: I guess maybe not. My therapist keeps saying that I bring a lot of my problems on myself by being a blaming kind of person and then feeling guilty about doing it.

P: Well, I don't know if your illnesses are "all in your head" or anything like that, but I do agree with the idea that nobody else is punishing you with them.

> *N: OK, I'll go along with that. But it still scares me to realize that God isn't forgiving me yet for all the terrible things I've done and I do in my life. And won't until I start forgiving those people.*

Forgiveness seems little more to Nora than a new form of righteousness according to the Law, whose specifics are set out in rules for securing God's approval. To Patsy, Nora's lack of a lively sense of grace and mercy threatens to defeat her best efforts to help the anguished parishioner see God's expectations from a broader perspective. She wonders whether Nora will ever recover from the spiritual myopia that is crippling her growth in faith. Like several other members of her congregation, Nora misperceives the Christian life in terms of the very legalism that infected Pharisaic Judaism in Jesus' time, a disease that he gave his life to heal. Theirs is the same kind of distorted vision that Peter displayed to Jesus in proposing to restrict forgiveness to multiples of seven. Chiding ourselves for failing to follow a fixed rule about forgiveness is sometimes easier than facing our responsibility to love our neighbors no matter how or how much they wrong us.

The fundamental problem with ignoring the context of Jesus' command to forgive is that it makes captive to his words the spirit that flows through them. Construing the obligation to be forgiving as merely one more duty to fulfill, one more rule to follow—or else—weakens drastically the power of any act of forgiveness to bring about genuine reconciliation. It substitutes for a faith buoyed by grace and peace one weighed down by obligations and the resentment that inevitably accompanies having to meet them.

Jesus on Forgiveness: The Larger Context

In discussing a variety of texts from the Gospels in which Jesus speaks specifically and emphatically about the obligatory nature of forgiveness, the previous section alluded to a larger context for his statements and insisted that only by looking at the statements against this background can we understand the true meaning of his words. This section attempts to characterize the wider context for understanding what otherwise seems to be a puzzling overstatement on Jesus' part, in conflict with his central message of a forgiving God whose love for us is in no way conditional upon how successful we are in fulfilling our obligations under the Law. The basic question for which we will be seeking an answer is: How is Jesus' statement, to the effect that God's forgiveness of us is dependent upon our forgiveness of others, not merely an imposition of a new law?

The beginning of an answer to this question is to be found earlier in the same Sermon on the Mount, which contains the Lord's Prayer, in Matthew 5:20: *For I tell you, if your virtue goes no deeper than that of the scribes and Pharisees, you will never get into the kingdom of heaven* (JB). Here, Jesus is calling his followers to a righteousness that is to exceed that of even the most faithful followers of the laws of Judaism. Its form is quite different from that with which the scribes and Pharisees are familiar, even though at one level it does not annul "even the least of the law's demands" (5:19). These demands, Jesus says, are still in force and deserving of both respect and obedience. However—and this is his main point—even if we were to fulfill every demand set forth in the more than six hundred prohibitions and commands considered binding upon Jews during Jesus' lifetime, we would still fall short of the kind of righteousness that he asks all who put their whole trust in him to emulate.

The virtue that goes deeper than that of the scribes and Pharisees is not a virtue shaped by more rigorous adherence to the Law's rules. It is, rather, a virtue formed by the spirit of the Law itself. Just what this spirit is Jesus reveals in replying to a Pharisee's question about which of the Law's commandments is the greatest. *Love the Lord your God with all your heart, with all your soul, and with all your mind,* Jesus says and then goes on to state a second commandment carrying a weight equal to the first: *Love your neighbor as yourself* (Matt. 22:37, 39 REB). The importance of this brief encounter becomes most apparent in the way that it ends, not with Jesus' offering a direct answer to a direct question, but with his changing the very terms of the question itself: *On these two commandments hang the whole Law, and the Prophets also* (v. 40 JB). The significance of what Jesus says to his questioner in these concluding words is beyond calculation. An old order of righteousness is passing away; a new form of existence in the world is breaking in before our very eyes.

Although Matthew presents the Pharisee's questioning of Jesus as an attempt to set a trap (22:35), there was nothing out of the ordinary about his question itself. It was common teaching in Jesus' day that all of the specific expectations and rules contained in the Law are anchored in, or arise from, a much smaller number of more basic, overarching commandments. Anyone who either claimed to be or was recognized as a teacher of the Law, therefore, could rightly expect to be asked about his understanding of just what these more basic commandments were. The Pharisee's asking Jesus about which commandments in the Law have priority is somewhat like today's philosophers asking one another what the ethical principles are that provide the rational foundation for more detailed codes of moral behavior. In both cases, the concern is with what lies behind specific rules for conduct, what the rules' underlying basis is, and how we justify holding people responsible for obeying one set of rules and not another.

If the particular question with which Matthew began his rendering of the Great Commandment is altogether ordinary in content and form, the way that Jesus answered it is not. In his declaration that the Law in its entirety, and the prophetic tradition that helps to interpret it, together rest upon a single foundation of love—of God, neighbor, and self—Jesus clearly intends to express a new understanding of righteousness altogether. It is an understanding that focuses directly, intensely, and steadfastly on foundations and not on the endlessly proliferating prohibitions and commandments that the foundations support. The deeper virtue (in Matt. 5:20) he envisions is based not on conformity to every nuance of an ever-expanding Law, but on love and love alone. Righteousness is not a matter of accumulating credits through legalistic observances. It is a matter of expressing gratitude for mercies tendered and of making personal sacrifices to show respect and care for others. We are creatures of God sunk in guilt not because we fail to behave according to the rules, but because we do not love God, others, and ourselves as God loves us.

Surprisingly, given the scope of the opposition to Jesus' ministry at its end, at least some people who were knowledgeable about the Law, and who listened to Jesus talk about this deeper virtue, seem to have appreciated what he said during his lifetime. In Mark's version of the conversation, for example, a scribe asks Jesus about which of the commandments comes first. After hearing Jesus' answer, the scribe praises what Jesus says and concludes by drawing an interesting contrast between loving God, neighbor, and self and making burnt offerings and sacrifices (Mark 12:33). Luke's account of the scene reverses the roles of Jesus and his questioner. Here, a lawyer who asks Jesus about inheriting eternal life is in turn asked by Jesus what the Law says. The lawyer's response, in the words of the Great Commandment, receives Jesus' approval (Luke 10:25-28). The dialogue then turns to a clarification of who our neighbor is by means of the revered parable of the good Samaritan.

Unlike Mark, Matthew and Luke portray the motive of Jesus' interlocutor as dishonest. In both their accounts, the principal aim is to provoke Jesus to say something that will justify Jewish authorities' mounting hostility toward him. Even so, they must have gone away empty-handed. For the articulation of the "greatest" of the commandments, Jesus merely reiterates the first commandment of the Decalogue, drawing upon Deuteronomy 6:4-5. Leviticus 19:18 is the basis of his second and equally binding commandment. No faithful Jew would have had any difficulty with the idea that these two commandments are of high, and even highest priority among all the prohibitions and positive commands in the Torah.

It is worthy of further reflection, then, that Jesus' vision of a deeper virtue won acceptance by some of the very people whose righteousness his vision undermined, particularly since the scribes and Pharisees as a group played so important a role in his humiliation and death. How, in particular, could the questioner in Mark's account, who surely must have been representative of more teachers of the Law than just himself, have possibly praised Jesus as lavishly as he did? On the basis of what understanding of Jesus' words could the questioner's affirmation have rested? More than likely, on the basis of an understanding that he wrongly attributed to Jesus, to the effect that the foundational principles of all the hundreds of prohibitions and commands of Jewish orthodoxy are made most fully manifest by our faithful obedience to each and every specific law in our daily lives.

According to this understanding, held by more than a few teachers of the Law in Jesus' lifetime, we show our love for God, neighbor, and self by striving to avoid everything that is prohibited, and to do everything that is commanded by the Law. *Everything*. There is no other way to honor the two greatest commandments except by honoring all the other ones, to the letter. In this light, it is somewhat ironic that while it is in Matthew's Gospel more than Mark's or Luke's that we are told how little the scribes and Pharisees grasped of Jesus' teaching about righteousness, it is also this same Gospel that goes to such lengths to assure us that the force of all the laws in the Law is still very much intact.

In fact, however, Jesus transforms Jewish law completely. He brings it to its perfection (Matt. 5:17) precisely by subordinating all of its prohibitions and commands—comprehensible only by the very learned, if at all—to the one, overarching, universally clear, unalterable, eternal decree of God that we must love him with all our heart, soul, and mind, and that we must love our neighbors and ourselves as the principal expression of our love for God. Two, and only two, commandments are necessary. And they are inseparable: We cannot love God with our whole being without also loving our neighbors and ourselves, namely, without loving everything that God also loves. What alone is essential to life in the kingdom of heaven, then, is love—not "sweet love," but sacrificial love—expressed in concrete actions toward God and toward everyone and everything in the created order. Set alongside this Great Commandment, every other statute, law, rule, duty, moral code, ethical system, and worldview becomes secondary in importance—distantly secondary.

Jesus' God-inspired vision of a virtue deeper than that of the scribes and Pharisees supplants their understanding of God's expectations in still another way. The twofold Great Commandment not only supersedes all other prohibitions and commands in the Torah, but also changes the very form of our relationship with the One who is its ultimate source. Being enjoined to love certainly involves being put under an obligation to behave in certain ways, and in this sense fulfilling the Great Commandment bears some resemblance to acting in accordance with a law or moral rule. But much more is involved than this. The "love commandment" is also—and more important—a call to become a different kind of person, namely, a willing servant to others rather than a self-centered pursuer of personal interests and well-being only.

Obeying the Great Commandment requires more of us than doing what we are required to do, while ignoring the negative feelings that sometimes accompany our doing so. "Going through the motions" cannot yield genuinely loving acts. Love requires caring and not reluctant engagement, commitment shaped by respect and concern for others' genuine well-being, person-centeredness more than rule-centeredness, and mercy and kindness instead of judgment and blame. The deeper virtue to which it points is not the virtue of outwardly conforming to rules, no matter how well conceived and just the rules may be. For Jesus, virtue is an inward excellence of character, whose spirit is manifest in every act that flows from it. The sacrificial love, which is its divinely intended expression, begins with trusting in God's forgiving our own wrongdoing and grows as we share gratefully and joyfully his forgiveness by becoming more forgiving of others.

The fundamental point of this section is that what Jesus said about our obligation to forgive must be read in the larger context of everything else that he taught about a virtue deeper than that of the scribes and Pharisees. From the standpoint of this larger context, the one thing that his summons to be unconditionally forgiving cannot mean is that by offering forgiveness to those who wrong us, and that only by doing so, we will win something from God that we do not already have. Precisely because Jesus gave his life as a ransom for many (Matt. 20:28), we are not left to our own devices to find relief from the guilt of our wrongdoing. Before we even think to ask for God's forgiveness, we are already forgiven sinners; forgiving others is the way of sharing in God's reconciling work in the world, not of earning something for ourselves only. As Jesus said to a paralyzed man: *Courage, my son! Your sins are forgiven* (Matt. 9:2 TEV) He asked nothing of the man in advance. As he said to others seeking rest for their souls: *Come unto me all ye that labour and are heavy laden, and I will give you rest. Take my yoke upon you, and learn of me. . . . For my yoke is easy, and my burden is light* (Matt. 11:28, 30 KJV). He asked nothing of them in advance. What he asks in return for mercies already tendered is a commitment to put others' needs first, from a love that begins and ends in forgiveness.

A Little More About Nora

Earlier in this chapter, a vignette illustrated a troubling spiritual condition that faithful Christians commonly experience. In the vignette, Nora tells her pastor, Patsy, about resentments that both agree are justifiable. Her dilemma is, though there are good reasons for her anger, she also believes (rightly) that God wants her to give up "nursing" it (Matt. 5:22 REB) and (wrongly) that until she does, God will withhold forgiveness of her sins and leave her with illnesses as punishment for her recalcitrance. After Patsy began challenging the global quality of Nora's self-denunciation, their conversation proceeded as follows:

> *P: Let's see if I understand you right. Your illnesses aren't God's doing, but you've still got some painful guilt feelings—and some scare besides—because you believe God hasn't forgiven you lots of past sins?*

N: Well, when you put it that way, I guess the guilt I feel is just for being so resentful about my present circumstances.
P: You've gotta forgive those people; you can't; and God will start putting heat on you until you do.
N: That's about it.
P: But, Nora, doesn't that make what Jesus said about forgiveness into just one more rule that we have to obey? Didn't he come to show us a way out of all this rules business?
N: I'm not sure what you're getting at.
P: What I'm getting at is that forgiveness isn't a do-it-or-else kind of thing. It's a way of becoming more loving in our hearts, just the way God is loving toward us.
N: (After considerable silence) *My God, Patsy, do you know what you're telling me? It isn't enough that I can't act like God wants me to act. Now I can't be the kind of person God wants me to be, and hearing this is supposed to make me feel better?*
P: I don't think God expects anyone to be perfectly loving all the time. What he asks is that we strive to be, with his help.
N: The one thing that I am "striving" to be, as you put it, is to be just that. But I'm not making it, Patsy, I'm not making it.
P: One step at a time, Nora, just one step at a time.

At one level, Nora's reaction to Patsy serves as a poignant reminder to all Christian caregivers that even the soundest of suggestions requires proper timing in order to be effective. Patsy moved a little too quickly to help Nora get beyond her works-righteousness mentality. Sooner or later, of course, she must confront Nora in something like the way she does here if she is to provide the kind of spiritual guidance that Nora so desperately needs. Clearly, though, Nora is not yet ready for the challenge, and Patsy's raising it later rather than sooner might have proved to be the better course to follow. With most of her friends pushing her to "get over it" and get on with her life, and with Patsy fighting the temptation to tell her the same thing, it is little wonder that Nora both craves and deserves more assurance, that it is all right to feel as angry as she feels. More constructive ways of dealing with the anger, and the guilt she feels harboring it, can come later.

At a deeper level, the content of Nora's reaction takes us close to the heart of one of the most difficult spiritual problems that every Christian faces many times during the struggle to become a more faithful follower of Jesus Christ: overcoming entrenched resistance to both offering and accepting forgiveness. Part of the problem is that, by God's grace, we know at the core of our being that guilt from wrongdoing is finally healed only by forgiveness, by our forgiving others and their forgiving us, whether on the basis of making amends or of being absolved from doing so. The other part of the problem is that wrongdoing—our own and others'—makes us vulnerable to feelings of anxiety, anger, guilt, shame, and despondency that can overwhelm all of our best intentions to heal the guilt that goes with it by means of constructive action flowing from a forgiving spirit. Overcoming resistance to being forgiving and forgiven, by dealing with the feelings that feed the resistance, is the vital center of all pastoral care—clergy and lay—to the guilt-ridden and the guilt-oblivious. How to render such care, to ourselves and to others, is the subject of the next chapter.

Summary

By our wrongdoing, we have incurred debts and obligations to God and to all others whom we have wronged. However, God, who has every right to hold our every debt against us, freely chooses to bestow mercy upon us instead, for the sake of reconciliation both on earth and in heaven. Like God, we, when wronged by others, have every right to hold the hurtful consequences of their wrongdoing against them. Also like God, however, we have the freedom to exercise mercy rather than judgment toward others, just as they have the freedom to be merciful toward us when we do harm to them. Whenever we or they choose mercy over judgment, God is made more fully manifest in the world, and God's work of reconciliation continues. Whenever we or they choose blame over mercy, though, God's presence in the world is obscured, and enmity takes the place of love in our relationships, including the relationship with our Creator.

CHAPTER SEVEN

FORGIVING OTHERS, FORGIVING OURSELVES: REMOVING THE OBSTACLES

Why is it that even strongly committed Christians sometimes hold on to resentments toward others, blame themselves for sins long forgiven, and feel guilty about both the resentments and the self-blame? Every wrong that we and others have committed "by thought, word, and deed against the divine majesty" and against our neighbors has been forgiven by the same God who calls us, as forgiven sinners, to forgive others as we forgive ourselves. Why, then, do we act as if we do not believe this fundamental truth with our whole hearts or even at all? What gets in the way of our accepting and sharing God's grace in the ways we know we should? The purpose of this chapter is twofold: (a) to bring clearly into view just what the obstacles are that impede our experiencing and sharing a grace-filled life, and (b) to show how to help people—ourselves included—overcome them.

Overcoming the Obstacles to Forgiving Others

In the vignette that the previous chapter left unfinished, Nora is struggling with guilt over not being able to forgive people she believes responsible for her present financial state. She is angry over their uncaring decisions about her child's medical expenses and fearful that God will not forgive her own unforgiving spirit. With her pastor's help, she has come to see that her own recent illnesses are not God's doing. If they are in any sense punitive in nature, they reflect a need to punish herself, if not for the failure to be a forgiving person, then for something else. The conversation between Nora and Patsy continues as follows:

> N: *Maybe you're right, Patsy. Maybe I am too hard on myself for not being a one hundred percent forgiving person. I guess I'd be willing to settle for a little lower grade on my spirituality for a while, if I just knew what to do first to start raising it.*
> P: *If you'll promise me not to take too literally the idea that God's grading you, I do think I've got an idea about how to start being that forgiving person you say you're not.*
> N: (Smiling) *I promise. But please don't tell me I have to give up my works righteousness right away; I'm not quite ready to do that yet!*
> P: *You're on!*

N: OK, Holy One. What do I do first?
P: Well, for starters, I want you to take a minute and bring to mind some time in your life when you received forgiveness you didn't deserve.

Patsy's invitation to Nora reflects both wisdom and a good sense of timing. It affirms Nora's reluctant acknowledgment that faith requires something more than clinging to expectations of divine retribution fine-tuned to each particular spiritual failing, and that the heart of faith is gratitude, not bitterness. Further still, Patsy's request carefully builds upon Nora's willingness to entertain the notion that spiritual growth is a step-by-step process and not one giant leap to perfection.

The strategy upon which Patsy is now embarked is one of encouraging Nora to change the focus of her attention away from judging herself in accordance with deeply entrenched, unhelpful beliefs, and toward reexperiencing moments of being enveloped by grace, mercy, and kindness rather than judgment, rejection, and punishment. Patsy's hope is that Nora's recollections will prove a sufficient challenge to the beliefs that are suffocating her sense of God's love. This strategy stands firmly on sound foundational principles of effective pastoral practice. Not surprising, therefore, Patsy is momentarily taken aback at Nora's response to her skillfully articulated guidance:

N: (After an uncomfortably long pause, and with tears welling up in her eyes) *As God is my witness, Patsy, all I ever got growing up was just one episode after another of criticism, judgment, getting blamed, being threatened, never doing things right. I know you're looking for me to say something else, and I want more than anything to do it, not just for you, but also for me. But—oh, Jesus, Jesus, Jesus* (Nora is crying now)—*that's all there is. That's all there is.*
P: (After her own long pause, during which she silently asks God to help her say the right thing, especially in the next moment) *Nora, now I think I know why it's been so hard for you to be forgiving. You can't remember ever*

experiencing forgiveness from the very people you most deserved to get it.
N: But that doesn't let me off the hook, Patsy. I'm supposed to be forgiving, no matter what I did or didn't get for myself.
P: I know, Nora, and I'm not trying to change your mind in any way about that, but I also believe, that just like love, forgiveness is harder to give when you don't think you've gotten your fair share of it yourself.
N: I'll sure go along with that. But look, Patsy, I've already slipped on only your first step. What do I do now?
P: How about standing on that step just a little longer?
N: Like how?
P: Like this: We've never talked about the awfulness of growing up under such criticism; I want you to get into the feelings you have about it.
N: Being mad and sad?
P: If that's what they are.

Patsy adjusts quickly to the conversation's unexpected turn. Sensing that Nora wants her to play a blame game with her against overly critical family members, she subtly reframes what Nora has said about growing up. Instead of responding to a distraught reminiscence as if it were an accurate account of her early life as a whole, Patsy construes it as a first and partial summary of how Nora in her present distress is remembering and thinking about some of the things that did and did not happen to her. Rather than taking the summary statement at face value, then, she communicates respect for and empathy toward Nora's recollections as recollections, namely, *You can't remember ever experiencing . . .*

Patsy chooses this response because she is convinced that Nora cannot have become the caring person that she is without experiencing somewhere the kind of forgiving and sacrificial love that she pours out in abundance to her children, to many of her family members and friends, and to her church. Patsy knows, however, that Nora must discover its truth for herself. Patsy still cringes recalling to mind what one otherwise well-intentioned church member recently said to Nora after a church service: *You need to be more respectful of your folks; I'm sure they tried their best, and I'll bet they showed they loved you in all sorts of ways.* And so, Patsy opts for gently encouraging Nora to reflect on her negative memories some more, hoping that by doing so she will begin to discover some positive ones besides. But Nora continues to resist:

N: All I'd be doing is whining, and nobody wants to hear that.
P: I think what you'd be doing is putting words to feelings that are down there pretty deep and that you hope will just stay there.
N: It's not that I don't know they're there. I do know they're there, and I feel terrible that they are.
P: Do you think you could be feeling this kind of "terrible" for a reason?
N: A reason? For God's sake, what?
P: Maybe for the sake of pushing you to get the feelings out, looked at, and put behind you.
N: But I don't want to get into them all over again. I've spent half my life trying to get over them.
P: That, I'm not so sure about.
N: What do you mean?
P: I could be way off base, Nora, but maybe your making yourself feel so guilty is a way of not dealing with them?
N: I'd rather feel guilty than feel all the other stuff?
P: That sounds a little strange to you.
N: More than just a little strange. But you know what? It also sounds right. 'Cause I sure enough haven't put those old feelings behind me, have I? And no matter how guilty I make myself feel about having them, they really haven't gone away.
P: It's a funny thing, isn't it, how we can get so out of whack over guilt. The whole idea behind guilt is that we make the changes we need to make in order to get rid of it. And lo and behold, sometimes we wind up storing the guilt itself and making no changes at all.

N: Now Patsy, you just know what I'm going to do with that idea! I'm going to start feeling guilty about not using my guilt feelings right.
P: (Chuckling) *Well, just make sure you do a good job of it.*

During a follow-up session with Patsy a week later, Nora shared several painful experiences of harsh judgments received during her early teenage years, along with the resentments harbored about them ever since. Whenever she began to blame herself for the resentments, Patsy reminded her that there is nothing wrong with feeling angry about injustices suffered. The conversation concluded as follows:

N: Talking about some very bad moments hasn't been as wrenching as I thought it would be. I'm grateful to you for being so patient with me.
P: I haven't been in any hurry, Nora. Perhaps, though, you're beginning to think that you've talked enough about them, at least for a while.
N: I do have a sense of—I guess that it's relief. But it surprises me a little. My therapist has tried to teach me that accepting certain feelings as OK will help me express them more openly and more often.
P: Sounds like solid advice to me.
N: I think so, too. But maybe there's something else about it, too.
P: Say more.
N: Right now, I don't feel guilty about being judged so much, and I don't feel much need to stay angry about it either.
P: Getting into at least those feelings has gotten you thinking about moving on from them.
N: Yeah. Maybe the thing to do is just accept that being judged happened a lot in my life, that I'm a little sad about it, but that that's just the way it was.
P: To me, that kind of acceptance will be easier to deal with than all the resentment and guilt you've been carrying around. I'm struck, though, with your saying that being

judged happened "a lot." Might that mean that it didn't happen at least sometimes?
N: I did say it that way, didn't I? Geez, Patsy, are we back to what I flunked earlier, remembering my being forgiven and not being judged?
P: Want a retest?
N: I think I just might be ready to pass it this time.

And "pass it," Nora did. With Patsy's further encouragement, she soon brought to mind two especially significant encounters with her father, quite different from those she had been repeating over and over in her mind. One was over damaging a valuable piece of farm equipment she carelessly drove into a creek. The other was over letting her high school extracurricular activities get in the way of her winning a college scholarship:

N: What I deserved for those screwups was a bunch of kicks in my rear end and grounding for years.
P: And what did you get?
N: Well, for my driving escapade, all my father did was say that accidents can happen to anybody and would I bring our big truck down to the creek and help him pull the tractor out of the muck.
P: He chose to call it an accident, when you both knew better.
N: Yep. And the grades thing blew me away even more. Both he and my mom told me that they loved all the stuff I did in high school—cheerleaders, 4-H, the whole nine yards—and that we'd work out the college money somehow.
P: Wow.
N: I guess that's the only thing to say about it.

Clearly, Patsy's pastoral guidance has proved highly effective. She began by reminding Nora of how hard it is, spiritually, to give what we have not ourselves received, even though she strongly believes that Nora received more of what she should be giving than she has allowed herself to be aware of. Then, Patsy reinforced Nora's conviction that she should be forgiving, whether she has personally experienced forgiveness or not, trusting that Nora will begin to find it easier to forgive others, the more she brings to mind instances of receiving forgiveness in her own life. The trust was well placed.

Patsy's interventions on Nora's behalf are grounded in an assumption that is sound both psychologically and theologically: Forgotten feelings, clinging to remembered offenses as barnacles cling to the undersides of boats, are a principal impediment to our forgiving both the original offenders and those who offend us in the present. Though we may feel guilty for not being more forgiving, the guilt we feel about our failure will not by itself lead us to a forgiving stance, unless we also deal with previously unexamined feelings of resentment and sadness over past offenses against us. Only when these feelings are acknowledged, accepted, and gradually relinquished can guilt begin to do its proper work.

Not everyone troubled enough by guilt to seek help for it is ready from the outset to follow the most reliable path through it. When Nora resisted Patsy's first invitation to remember moments of grace in her life, Patsy did not back away from her faith-driven conviction that there were in fact such moments, no matter how far out of awareness Nora may have driven the memory of them. But neither did she argue the point with Nora. Instead, Patsy respected Nora's need to dwell for a while longer on the negative side of her upbringing, trusting that the more validated Nora felt in the negative feelings themselves, the sooner she would be ready to move on from them. Patsy's strategy proved successful.

What can we learn about forgiveness and the healing of guilt from Patsy's very caring and competent ministry to her guilt-ridden church member, Nora? First, that feeling guilty over not being able to forgive is precisely what we are supposed to feel, when we withhold offering what God constantly offers us. Whether it is attributed to conscience or to the spirit of God, or both, feeling guilty about being unforgiving serves the purpose of goading us to let go of still other feelings that keep us alienated from those who wrong us. The feelings that we particularly need to get behind us are resentments over wrongs done to us in the past and sadness about being a victim of others' wrongdoing rather than a recipient of others' benevolence.

The second thing that we can learn from Patsy and Nora is that we have a responsibility to put and keep both our resentments and our sadness in perspective. First, either is an appropriate reaction to being repeatedly judged too harshly. Second, both can and do get in the way of understanding people realistically. Not everyone forgives us easily, but not everyone harbors resentments toward us either, even when they have good reason to do so. As a whole, our experiences include encounters with both kinds of people, just as they include receiving judgmental as well as compassionate responses from the same people in different situations. Which encounters and which responses we will remember most clearly is finally a matter of choice and not necessity.

The pastoral care that Patsy offered Nora aimed especially at strengthening her God-given capacity to make choices, by helping her recover some uplifting memories of being forgiven and put them alongside her many painful memories of being called to account and found wanting. As is the case with all good pastoral care, Patsy's yields a mixed blessing to its recipient. On the one hand, Nora has been comforted by discovering that she is a subject not only of others' criticism, but also of love, the kind of love whose basis and transforming power is forgiveness. On the other hand, she can no longer excuse her own unforgiving spirit by blaming it on the mercilessness of others. Even more, she can no longer claim to atone for it by feeling miserable about not overcoming it. Remembering what she now is remembering—judgment *and* mercy—Nora must choose which set of memories she will draw upon from this point on to shape her basic outlook toward herself, other people, and God. The Holy Spirit, working through the deepening relationship between Patsy and Nora, is putting before Nora a way of becoming a more forgiving—and resilient—person by inviting her to take the good along with the bad.

Forgiving Others As We Forgive Ourselves

The primary obstacle to forgiving people who wrong us in the present is harboring grudges against people who have wronged us in the past. Insisting that others owe more to us than they deserve to receive from us hinders seriously the development of a forgiving spirit. What makes the insistence so difficult to deal with is that it roots in feelings of resentment and sadness about injustices suffered long ago rather than in reactions to offenses in the here and now. It undermines remembering others' kindness and fixates instead on others' criticisms. It pushes us to treat others in terms of harsh accountability, unrelenting judgment, and swift punishments instead of in terms of patience, understanding, and going the second mile. Even worse, it offers no solace when, in the name of a more genuine faith, we must acknowledge our guilt about being so resentful and sad in the first place.

All of these considerations are germane to the other side of becoming a more forgiving person: forgiving ourselves. Often in my ministry, people confess to me that they have done something they should not have done, or failed to do something that they should have done, and that they are overcome with guilt about it. In more than just a few instances, the person with whom I am talking will go on to say things like the following:

> *Sally says she forgives me for the affair, but how could she? I've been cheating on her for months, lying to her about it, trashing her in my mind so I could feel better about what I was doing. If I can't forgive myself, why should she forgive me? I don't deserve her, pastor; I don't deserve her.*

> *Jimmy was right. I favored his brother over him all the time the boys were growing up, and I wouldn't listen to him when he tried to tell me. He's such a loving and caring man now, no thanks to me. All he wants from me is to let go of feeling bad for being such a lousy mother to him. I only wish I could.*

> *When I didn't blow the whistle on what they were doing in the company, I felt that I let down everybody who tried to teach me all my life the difference between right and wrong. And worst of all, I let Christ down; he died for his beliefs, while I acted like mine just weren't all that important. But he forgave me! He forgave me! Yet here I am, feeling guilty as sin again, with no relief in sight.*

People who make statements like these are desperately in need of empathy and encouragement, if they are ever to move beyond self-blame toward accepting grace that is already theirs. They do not need to hear from well-meaning Christian friends words like these:

> *You've done everything that any human being could possibly do to make it up to her. So even if she is still holding it against you, we both know that God isn't. I don't see how you can be the Christian I know you are and still hold on to this much guilt. Let me say it again: In the name of Jesus Christ, you're forgiven! OK?*

This statement is a good example of conveying a profound truth, but one that is unhelpful to the situation at hand. Certainly, as faithful Christians, we are not supposed to carry around unnecessary burdens of guilt. Instead, we are called to share with others God's glorious and unmerited acts of grace that we experience constantly in our lives. The problem is that (a) even though we know this to be true, we can find it hard to forgive ourselves for what others have already forgiven us, and (b) in spite of everything we know about grace as a sheer gift, we can also feel guilty for not accepting it when it is freely offered to us. This spiritual dilemma arises not because we fail to understand our faith correctly; we understand it all too well. Therefore, it does not help merely to be pressured to do what we already know we should be doing. What helps is patient understanding and support, while we try to discover what prevents us from claiming others' forgiveness with joy.

Basically, we refuse to forgive ourselves because we believe that the forgiveness we have in fact received is forgiveness that we have not deserved. What lies behind this belief, surprisingly, is audacity. Grandiose in our sense of worthlessness, we callously toss self-denunciations in the face of anyone—God included—whom we take to be misguided enough to say something positive about us in spite of the wrongs we have committed. Stung by such presumptuousness, even the most patient family member, friend, or caregiver may be tempted to push back somewhat aggressively, for example, *You've got to stop talking like this—now!*

A better way of dealing with feelings of rejection when our best caring efforts are discounted would take the form of a confrontation, not in the sense of denunciation, but in the sense of invitation. In specific, we might invite the self-blaming person to reflect on the contradiction between (a) believing that all of us are indeed forgiven sinners and (b) discounting forgiveness from God and others in his or her own case. As valid and appropriate as it may be, however, the invitation can easily fail if it is heard as a preemptive effort on our part to get him or her out of a state of misery as quickly as possible, because we ourselves are uncomfortable with it. The truth does indeed set us free, but rarely all at once and almost never until we are ready to hear it. Pressuring self-blaming people to confront their audaciousness honestly is not likely to motivate positive change unless, somehow and at the right moment, whatever pressure we may apply can be applied in love. How this can be accomplished is the subject of the vignette to follow.

Raised in a series of neglectful and abusive foster homes, Bud entered adolescence with a chip on both of his shoulders, a mountain of trust issues, a penchant for taking what he wanted when he wanted it, and an annoying knack for escaping arrest. At sixteen, he barely survived an automobile accident from drag racing. The second afternoon in the hospital, he awoke to a whispered conversation across the room between another patient and a priest, Father Dan. Before leaving the room, the priest spoke briefly with Bud, successfully initiating a pastoral relationship that continued long after Bud's release. Eventually, with his

Parish Council's enthusiastic support, Father Dan provided Bud with a room on the grounds, a job with the parish's sexton, mentoring during his struggles to finish high school, a recommendation to the local Catholic college, and, still later, his blessing when Bud wanted to marry a young woman from the parish.

Late one afternoon, Father Dan looked through his office window to the courtyard outside and saw Bud leaning up against a tree, his gardening tools scattered randomly on the ground, tears streaming down his face. The priest quickly went out to determine what had happened. Part of the conversation that ensued went as follows:

> *Dan: Bud, Bud, what's wrong?*
> *Bud: Nothing's wrong, Father, nothing, just nothing. Thanks to you, everything in my life has been going just great for a long time. And that's the problem!*
> *D: I guess you're going to have to explain that one to me a little.*
> *B: I know it sounds crazy, Father. You pulled me out of a big pit, made me feel like I had a family for the first time in my life. And now I've got a future, and here I am, standing here acting like I'm ungrateful for all of it. I'm not ungrateful, Father, I'm not. What all of a sudden is hitting me is that I don't deserve any of it.*
> *D: All of a sudden you just decided this?*
> *B: Yes, Father. Nobody came up to me and said it. If they did, I'd just throw it right back in their faces, like I did at school. I'm saying it to myself.*
> *D: How come you're looking at things this way now, and not at some other time? Any ideas?*
> *B: Maybe it's because I'm so in love with Millie and she's so well liked and all, and I've been worrying myself sick that she'll see me for what I really am, and then all the good stuff in my life will just go away.*
> *D: You've been chewing on not being good enough for Millie, and now you're not so sure you're good enough, period.*
> *B: It sounds stupid, Father, but it's the way I feel.*

Bud's life, from the time of his near fatal automobile accident to the present, is a success story in every sense of the term—in Father Dan's experience, a rare and much cherished success story. At an early stage in their relationship, the priest admitted to Bud: *I really didn't think I was getting very far with my offer to help, but I was praying every night that you wouldn't keep on being the angry kid you had every right to be.* And Bud admitted to the priest: *I knew you were, Father, and you were the only one who ever did. It got to me. Maybe it was because I never really wanted to be the loser that I was turning into. I wanted a way out, and you gave me one.* Most pastors and lay caregivers are likely to agree with Father Dan, that the results of Christian caring are not usually as dramatic as they proved to be with Bud. But it is precisely because the effect of this priest's ministry with Bud is so dramatic that his work is useful to the present discussion.

Although his spiritual problem with forgiveness and guilt is quite different from the one discussed earlier in the case of Nora, Bud shares with Nora many of the same kinds of experiences growing up that contribute to both problems. In particular, both Nora and Bud are victims of an enormous amount of neglect and abuse. What is especially interesting for our purposes is how differently each interprets the meaning of these experiences for the living of their lives in the present. Prior to her work with Patsy, Nora chose to see the whole of her upbringing in terms of undeserved criticism, with the result that her capacity to forgive others became crippled. Bud focused as narrowly on experiences of judgment as Nora did, but, unlike Nora, he chose to internalize them as expressing the whole truth about himself. The malignant result was a crippling of his capacity to forgive himself and to accept with gratitude others' kindnesses. Believing that she has long deserved better treatment herself, Nora cuts others no slack for their mistakes and wrongs. Believing that he deserved what he got then and that he deserves no better now, Bud resists the joy that comes with unmerited grace. Between the two, Bud has the deeper spiritual problem. While Nora's difficulty is with bringing to mind enough positive experiences of being forgiven for something, Bud's is with trusting he is really worthy of anyone's forgiveness and acceptance at all.

As he listened to Bud in the courtyard that afternoon, Father Dan experienced a flood of mixed feelings. He delighted in the progress Bud was making in accepting that his future could be rich and fruitful, in spite of the many transgressions of his earlier years. But he worried over how out of touch Bud still seemed to be with a touchstone of the faith that both of them had talked about many times, a faith that the priest understood by means of a theology of the image of God. Though Bud seemed to grasp the words, the meaning of the words still seemed to be eluding him: his created likeness to his Creator, and his Creator's (positive) image of him. Father Dan pondered how he might broach the subject without giving Bud one more thing for which to reproach himself, in this case, by making his lack of faith in himself a sign of lack of faith in God. After the two returned to the priest's study, Father Dan gently invited Bud to think about his self-reproaches in the light of his growing faith:

> *D: A few minutes ago you were saying that you don't deserve all the good things that are happening to you because you aren't worthy of them. Is that because of all the bad stuff you used to do?*
> *B: I'll never be able to make up for that bad stuff, but I guess I feel that until I do I'll never be the guy that Millie takes me for.*
> *D: You have to get your record cleaned up, and yet you'll never be able really to do it completely. Sounds like you can't win for losing.*
> *B: That is the way I'm seeing it, Father.*
> *D: And I respect that, Bud. I do. But is your way of looking at these things the only right one?*
> *B: Well, I know you've been on my case, trying to get me to feel better about myself, and I appreciate it. But you're a priest, and that's what you're supposed to do.*
> *D: Actually, I was thinking of someone else's perspective on you.*

B: If you're going to bring in God here, Father, I don't think it's going to help.
D: His opinion doesn't count?
B: It was easier a while back to think so. But now I guess I do know better.
D: Yeah, I think you do know better on that score. But what's getting to me is that you seem to be putting your own opinion on a pedestal above his.
B: Like believing that I'm pretty rotten when he doesn't?
D: Out of the mouth of a forgiven sinner!

In spite of Father Dan's fear, that he might put Bud off by challenging too strongly Bud's negativity toward himself, he wisely determined that some kind of challenge was called for at the moment and that framing the challenge explicitly in the language of their shared faith had the best hope of succeeding. The priest was right on both counts. In every way possible, our faith affirms both our freedom and our responsibility to think deeply and well about our experience; to analyze, question, surmise, and decide; and to construct a holistic perspective on things by using wisely our God-given abilities to do so. In the final reckoning, though, it is God's perspective that is the decisive one, not ours, and from that perspective, we do not have the right to burden those who care about us with the remembrance of wrongdoing long forgiven. Father Dan helped Bud arrive at this understanding by choosing well the moment for expressing a frustration: *But what's getting to me is . . .*

As Father Dan saw it, what guilt-ridden people most need to understand is that in spite of all their wrongdoing and wrongfulness, Jesus Christ died to restore the image of God in all of us and to reempower us to care for all of creation as good shepherds care for their flocks. Though he appreciated the importance of raising this understanding with Bud in a timely way, he also saw to it that Bud could neither avoid nor evade its implications. In our own conversations with guilt-ridden people, however and whenever we choose to remind them of God's all-surpassing love, remind them we must, for this is indeed the truth that finally breaks the power of self-blame.

Summary

This chapter has sought, first, to identify the major obstacles that get in the way of experiencing and sharing God's forgiving love. Then, with the help of two vignettes, the discussion turned to characterizing effective pastoral strategies for ministering to people who know that they should be more forgiving both of others and of themselves than they presently find it possible to be. Along with the preceding chapters, this present one has focused on the healing of guilt in one-on-one relationships jeopardized by wrongdoing on the part of one or each party to the relationship. Before this book can properly be brought to a close, however, the issue of pastoral care and the healing of guilt must be looked at from a perspective that focuses on more than the wrongs that one person perpetrates upon another. In specific, we also need to look at healing the guilt that accrues from wrongdoing inflicted by the Christian community itself. This is the subject of the next, and final, chapter.

Chapter Eight

The Church: Forgiving and Forgiven

This final chapter focuses on collective rather than individual guilt, and specifically on the guilt that Christian communities bear from wrongful acts of omission and commission against their own members. Two corollary concerns will be dealt with along the way: the failure of Christian communities to forgive people who have offended against them; and the inability of people wronged by other Christians to forgive the churches that permitted the wrongdoing. The primary purpose of the chapter is to show what pastoral leadership can mean in congregations struggling both with their own wrongdoing and with the hurt and resentment of those who are its victims.

Healing Guilt When the Church Is the Wrongdoer

Immediately upon entering the classroom, he saw her. While other class members were gathering around the refreshment table and chatting with one another, she sat in the back of the room, gazing out the window, fighting back tears. The young associate minister (Ned) could not get to her before the class president called things to order and then welcomed him warmly as the guest teacher for the morning. Ned's lesson was well received, but it was difficult for him to stay focused on it. He wanted to find out what was troubling this class member, and why he seemed to be the only one to notice her distress.

After class, Ned reached the young woman just before she left the room and asked if they might visit for a minute or two outside. Even though other classes were streaming out into the corridor by then, she began talking openly about the pain she felt, even before she told Ned her name (Alicia). Several minutes later, with the next hour of Sunday school beginning, Alicia interrupted herself in the middle of a sentence to ask: *Do you think I should go ahead and look for another class, like they obviously want me to?*

Alicia's class, Ned had believed, was one of the congregation's strongest. Her present experience in it, however, caused him to wonder. Alicia and her husband, Maury, two of the class's founding members, recently divorced. As Alicia told it, the divorce was initiated by Maury, who had fallen in love with another woman and wanted to be free to marry her. Although Maury left the church as soon as he had Alicia served with divorce papers, Alicia actively sought nurture from the members of the Sunday school class and was crushed by their responses. Most have turned cool toward her; one has openly asked what Alicia did "to drive a good man like Maury off," and another suggested to her before class began that both she and the members would be better off if she were to move on: *Divorce is not the kind of witness we feel our class should be making in the church.*

Ned saw in Alicia's question an openness to exploration and suggested a follow-up conversation the next afternoon at the church. Before their meeting, Ned did some homework on Alicia's class. Although the membership rolls had gaps, they helped him discover two things of importance to Alicia's situation. The first was that there seemed to be only one single person currently listed as a member, whom Ned knew to be widowed. The second was that two couples on earlier rolls were people the senior pastor reported as "missing in action" since their own divorces. Both discoveries gave Ned pause and presented him with two challenges.

Ned's first challenge was to deal adequately with Alicia's question about her Sunday school membership. He decided, wisely, to encourage Alicia to answer the question for herself, shared with her the data he uncovered, and invited her to think out loud about what it might mean for the long run to remain with the group or to leave it for another. It is Ned's second challenge that is the focus of this section: guiding the members of this Sunday School class toward (a) a clearer understanding of their attitudes toward divorced people; (b) developing greater empathy and compassion for members struggling with loss in their lives, of whatever kind; and (c) representing Christ's love to Alicia whether she returns to their fellowship or not.

From the start, Ned ran into difficulties meeting this second challenge. One of his fellow staff members tried to discourage him from taking on the challenge at all: *Ned, that class is a couples' class. It's got a right to be a couples' class; it's a good couples' class. Alicia should just move on. There are other places in the church for her.* Another staff member took exactly the opposite position: *Guys, this class is way off base and needs to be called out. Ned, go in there and read them the riot act.* Class officers were reluctant to put Ned's concerns on the table for the members' discussion at all: *All it'll do, Ned, is just make people get angry or feel guilty. We've got a great bunch of people here, and we don't need to get them all riled up.* And the senior pastor pointedly reminded Ned that the church's Sunday school classes pretty much do their own thing and that this is the reason their members are enthusiastic about the classes.

But Ned persisted. First, he confronted both of his peers' stances directly. He agreed with them that Sunday school classes should have wide latitude in forming their fellowships but insisted that class members should not determine all by themselves who else fits in and who does not. He expressed his own outrage at the class's behavior toward Alicia but went on to say he knew that merely beating up on its members will not help the situation. The kind of confrontation they need, Ned argued, is one that invites them to reflect seriously on the gap they have opened up between what they say about themselves as a Christian group and how they are living out what they say. Impressed with Ned's clarity, strong conviction, and pastoral sensitivity, the senior pastor gave Ned his blessing to "take on the group and help them see for themselves the better way." Finally, Ned refused to be put off by the class officers' first reaction to his concern. Basically, he made them an offer they neither could nor did refuse:

> *There's a chance that people in the class will resent my wanting to talk with them about something unpleasant, just when we're getting along so well. But folks, there's something going on here that doesn't look very healthy to me, and I think we all ought to try to figure out together what it is, so that we'll know what to do about it. That's all I want to try to get across. I'll be coming to listen, OK?*

Today, Alicia's Sunday school class is stronger because Ned accepted the challenge to help remind its members of what a truly Christian fellowship is. In doing so, the class discovered to its surprise what lay behind the coolness toward Alicia. One identified it insightfully as the "fear of contagion." *It sounds so stupid, Ned, and it is stupid, but I guess we've been afraid that the breakup of Alicia and Maury will somehow infect our own marriages.* In response to this remarkably candid self-disclosure, Ned risked asking further: *What do you think this might be saying about your marriages?* Several class members saw the point of Ned's question right away: *I guess we're more scared than we want to admit. Too scared even to be there for one of our earliest members when she needed us.* The discussion ended with a pledge to reach out to Alicia with heartfelt apologies and to implore her not to leave the group. The efforts at reconciliation were successful, due in no small measure to the speed and skill with which Ned acted to initiate them.

How to Make the Church's Guilt Even Worse

Almost everything that Ned did so effectively to help one group of Christians work through their collective guilt, another pastor failed to do for another group, with lasting harm to his church the result. Allen had been looking forward to attending the Men's Fellowship dinner meeting, his first in a while. Pausing for a moment before offering the invocation, he noticed how poor the attendance was. Over dinner, he asked the program chairman about the "off night" and was startled by the reply: *Preacher, we've had several off nights now, and I don't think things are going to get better anytime soon.* The two men agreed to talk more after the meeting.

What Allen learned from Milt, the program chair, was that at least eight members were dealing with serious financial problems occasioned by investing money in a failed scheme devised and misrepresented by one of the most likeable members of the class. Three of the eight were attempting to recoup some of their losses by persuading still other members to invest in the project themselves. *All these guys are just devastated, Allen, over a fellow Christian betraying them. That's why they aren't here. They're scared, they're angry, their wives are furious, and they think their church is responsible for their troubles because it allowed this predator to keep ripping people off.* The conversation between Allen and Milt continued as follows:

Allen: Milt, that's just crazy thinking. This church can't be responsible for these men throwing their money away so foolishly. They did it to themselves all on their own. There are fast talkers everywhere, even in our churches, I'm afraid. I wish it weren't so, but it is so.
Milt: Well, Allen, they and their families are leaving our church over this whole thing. Can't we find some way to stop them? Like coming down hard on the friend who sold them such a bill of goods?
A: I think they need to take their lumps and get over it. In the meantime, I could talk with the man who started all this and see if he has anything he might be willing to confess to me. You have to know, though, that that will be just between him and me; I couldn't talk with anyone else about what he says to me.
M: What about going to the men who've been hurt and at least offer them some words of encouragement?
A: You know, Milt, that sounds like a good idea, but if I follow through on it, we could be putting the church in harm's way. You've told me how angry they are, and maybe even desperate. If I acknowledge, as the pastor of this church, what's been done to them, I could be giving these men ammunition to use against us, maybe even to sue us with. After all, a lot of these deals were done in and around meetings here at the church.
M: I guess we've got to be on guard these days about everything, don't we?
A: You better believe it. There are just a lot of ways to get broadsided when you least expect it.

At a critical moment in the life of a fellowship highly valued by his congregation, Allen offered no reassurance to people victimized that anyone else cares about them. Worse still, he showed no inclination to create opportunities for guilt from wrongdoing to be acknowledged, atoned for, and forgiven. Unlike Ned, this shepherd chose to ignore some of his sheep's pain altogether, hoping that by doing so the rest of the flock would remain blind and deaf to what was going on, and that the fleeced would quietly find their way to pastures far removed from the one in which they were violated.

That the guilty parties in this distressing situation extend far beyond the swindler and a "wish-it-would-all-go-away" pastor is evident from the positions taken on the issue by key lay leaders who were warned by Allen of the possible trouble on the horizon:

> *Sure, nobody would really succeed in putting the blame on the church for allowing this guy to take advantage of other people the way he did, but that won't stop someone from trying. And it'll take up a lot of our time and energy if we have to deal with it.*
>
> *If these people are this dumb, then they better go someplace else, where somebody will just lead them by the hand. They deserve what they're getting. It's a tough old world out there, and the sooner they find that out, the better. This investment guy probably did them all a favor.*
>
> *Allen, after you deny him Communion, you ought to make that man stand up right in the worship service and read the riot act to him in front of everybody.*
>
> *Great idea! If these other guys want to take us to task, this would show all concerned that the church doesn't condone his behavior.*

These are truly appalling positions, self-serving and judgmental, unworthy of people who genuinely believe themselves to be faithful followers of Jesus Christ. Intending to keep one man's wrongful acts attached to him and him alone, church leaders instead multiplied the malignant effects of the acts exponentially by afflicting the people suffering from them with an even greater evil: abandonment by the very community of faith that calls all of its members to be agents of reconciliation to others.

In the aftermath of this crisis, many in the church blamed both the leaders of the Men's Fellowship and Allen for not protecting fellow members against this particular predator from the beginning. Others, arguing more realistically that *sometimes you don't see it coming until it hits you right in the face*, nevertheless faulted Allen for a disastrous cover-up of what they (rightly) believed should have been dealt with openly at the time of its discovery, at whatever pain to the congregation. Over Allen's protests, two in this latter constituency demanded and received from the congregation's trustees permission to reach out both to the victimizer and to the victimized in this situation, for the purpose of bringing about a reconciliation between themselves and the church.

Not surprising, the best efforts of these conscientious Christians yielded no positive results. Animosity in the Men's Fellowship was literally at the breaking point; many of its members were leaving the church with great bitterness over what had happened to them. Their financial losses were too extensive to be compensated for by the victimizer, even if he could have been convinced to make the effort. The fear of litigation continued to immobilize Allen and his lay leaders, for whom the financial risks to the congregation outweighed the opportunities for spiritual growth that accepting appropriate responsibility could have opened up. One legal expert's advice proved decisive:

> *Going for reconciliation means being willing to admit at least some responsibility, and in this situation it can be too downright expensive to admit even the possibility of responsibility. No, I don't think we can be held accountable, but it will simply cost us too much to prove it. We've got to lay low on this.*

Learning from Our Successes and Mistakes

From the sharply contrasting leadership styles of two pastors, Ned and Allen, there is much to be learned about the healing of collective guilt in the church. Ned's style is anchored by the historic principles of Christian pastoral care (a) that the whole community of faith bears responsibility when the sins of its members prove offensive or harmful to others and (b) that the reconciliation of sinners with those sinned against is a principal concern of the church's pastoral care—clerical and lay—at all times and everywhere. Reflecting these principles, Ned unhesitatingly intervened in the affairs of a Sunday school class about to ostracize a member in need and, with the support of fellow staff members and class leaders, called its members to confront openly their behavior in the light of their faith. The results included new insight, repentance, and reconciliation with a sister in Christ.

As forceful as Ned was in bringing this particular issue out into the open, he did not let his indignation override his pastoral instinct. He rightly saw the pastoral issues as twofold: Alicia's pain and her friends' fears. In order to deal effectively with the former, he knew that he had to deal with the latter at the same time. To this end, Ned approached Alicia's fellow class members not in a spirit of judgmentalism, but in a spirit of trust and puzzlement. In specific, he expressed aloud his trust of the class's commitment to being a loving fellowship in Christ's service. Then he offered for consideration his curiosity and confusion about behaviors that seemed to fly in the face of the members' manifest desire to bear witness to God's love everywhere. Finally, he invited class members to share their own observations, feelings, and thoughts about what was going on and why. By listening well, being honest about his own perceptions, and asking pertinent questions at the right times, Ned guided Alicia's lapsed friends to discover for themselves what he hoped they would see and to initiate appropriate actions on their own to restore their relationship with her.

In earlier times, it might have sufficed for a priest or pastor, exercising the power of the pastoral office itself, to demand a certain course of action on the part of offending groups within the church and to threaten punishments of various kinds if the demands were not met, for example, withholding the sacraments, assigning protracted acts of penance, barring participation, or even outright excommunication. Certainly, there are still situations that demand of the church and its pastors forceful responses like these, such as in the face of overt racism, gender discrimination, dissemination of demonstrably false teaching, subverting the church's mission and programs by clandestine means, willfully destructive acts, criminal behavior and its cover-up, and the like. In general, however, it is widely recognized today that compelling a change of heart by the exercise of power alone is less likely to bring about the desired result than inviting self-examination in an environment of support, grace, and prayerful encouragement. That the process of acknowledging communal guilt has undergone significant change, though, does not minimize the importance of the acknowledgment itself.

With Ned's patient guidance, Alicia's Sunday school class came to its senses before things became too far out of hand. Because the class did, Alicia's hurt feelings did not for very long stand in the way of forgiving her classmates and reuniting with them. For members of the Men's Fellowship in Allen's church, it was too late for good outcomes. Families that might have been willing earlier to consider forgiving, even if it meant losing precious resources to another's wily schemes, eventually closed their hearts completely to their church because its leaders persistently and perniciously refused to listen to their distress.

The blatant refusal of churches to listen for and deal with the pain they cause their members is a major source of eroding support for the institutional church today. It is a major reason that, for so many people, spirituality is "in" but religion is "out." To them, "religion" inevitably becomes captive to institutions, whose primary concern is self-protection and, wherever possible, the aggrandizement of its leaders, clergy, or lay. Allen's church illustrates well what many see in and fear from institutional Christianity in general. Faced with a genuine moral and spiritual crisis, its leaders allowed a cowardly retreat into silence and cover-up to replace compassion, the willingness to listen, and the courage to do the right thing. Their stonewalling is like that of institutional leaders who dealt with pedophile priests by hushing things up and transferring the offenders to other areas, only to discover that they commit the same offenses over and over again.

Stonewalling is not the only way that churches refuse to pay heed to those they wound. Nonstop haranguing is another. For example, zealous sects of all theological persuasions continue to pour scorn on people who profess a religion other than their own, on people who emphasize the right to life over the right to choose, on people who refuse to confront injustice with sufficient aggressiveness, on people who allow blood transfusions, on people who enter adulthood with what in their eyes is the wrong sexual orientation, on people who report spousal and child abuse to authorities outside their churches, on people who emphasize the right to choose over the right to life—in short, on anyone who fails to conform to their own warped ideas about the Christian life. Fulminating to everyone, they listen to no one. Ferreting out others' defects, they overlook others' wounds. Lost in wonder over their good intentions, they brook no criticism of their actions, caricaturing their critics as representatives of the evil it is their self-appointed mission to eradicate.

Could the Men's Fellowship of Allen's church have averted the crisis into which a member's manipulations plunged it? Possibly. As word of the group's travail gradually made its way through the congregation, for example, Allen discovered that several in the Fellowship had suspected for some time that the deals being done were fraudulent. Each man assumed their pastor knew of the mounting troubles and, as a consequence, did not bother to tell him. Had he known sooner, could he have done anything to improve the situation? Possibly. For one thing, he could have insisted, as Ned did, that all who are affected by a fellow Christian's sins share the responsibility to challenge the offending behavior and to seek reconciliation with the offender. Allen seemed to assume, instead, that sin is a matter for the pastor and not the members to handle.

There would have been still another way for Allen to act effectively on behalf of the stricken Men's Fellowship. His church's tradition includes a strong emphasis on the laity's seeking priestly absolution for sins. If his errant parishioner believed at all in the rightness and power of confession and penance, he might have been responsive had Allen pushed him to own up to what he did, express contrition for it openly, make whatever restitution he could, and seek forgiveness from the congregation whose trust he violated. However, Allen's personal penchant for avoidance could have led him to settle for a promise on the part of his penitent to get help for himself and not repeat the offending behaviors.

Dealing with Collective Guilt in the Church Today: Four Issues

Most pastors want to believe that dealing effectively with collective guilt in the church should be a relatively smooth process, once we understand a few basic principles and once we muster the courage to stay the course. That the process can so quickly become complicated and arduous, and its outcome less certain, can be frustrating to them. Of all the possible hindrances to reconciliation in congregations and church institutions, four in particular make the process of healing our churches' collective guilt especially difficult today: (1) the mutual projection of personal sins denied and disowned; (2) the privatizing of sin, repentance, and forgiveness; (3) the disenfranchising of laity from the ministry of forgiveness; and (4) the mutually exclusive relationship between a reconciling and a litigious spirit. This section, concluding both the chapter and the book, discusses what we must do about them.

Projection

An exercise in imagination: The fast-talking scam artist of Allen's church has had a change of heart. Realizing the error of his ways and the hurt he has caused, he approaches Allen to express an earnest desire to change for the better, with God's help, and to seek in every way possible to compensate members of the church for the damage he has caused them. Allen is impressed with the man's sincerity and, with him, believes that the Holy Spirit is genuinely at work remaking him in God's image. He shares with parish leaders and members of the Men's Fellowship a proposal for reconciliation that will include the congregation's surrounding its errant member with caring support as he accepts his just punishment under the law and seeks to rebuild his life after serving it. Allen is soundly rebuffed. If all this really had taken place in Allen's church, what might we make of it?

Most of us would likely accept the rebuff itself as a normal first reaction. The damage done is extensive, the feelings about it are intense, the pastor's empathy is uncharacteristic, and skepticism about the offender's genuineness is more than called for. However, if the initial rebuff reflects an already hardened heart on the part of Allen's congregation, there is less to accept and more to challenge. Allen's parishioners have good reason to be wary of the authenticity of this particular sinner's conversion and to hesitate taking the risks that their pastor is asking them to take. However, if their skepticism is tantamount to doubting or denying the possibility of conversion itself, it becomes something itself to be skeptical about.

As discussed earlier, a major reason that members of Allen's congregation cannot forgive is that their leaders allowed initial shock over betrayal to escalate to uncontrollable outrage. However, this reason cannot explain why the outrage could continue at the same level after reconciliation becomes genuinely possible. What alone can explain this latter is embedded in one of Jesus' most painful reminders, to the effect that we dwell on smaller defects of others more than we attend to massive ones of our own (Matt. 7:3). Jesus intended these words as an illustration of a larger point: *Judge not, that ye be not judged* (Matt. 7:1 KJV).

Literally speaking, swindling people out of money is more than having a speck, or a piece of sawdust, in one's eye. Symbolically understood, however, it is something far less than all of the sins together that Christians commit and would like to commit. The latter reference is especially important to the present discussion: The sins of others, that we will not allow ourselves to forgive, are more often than not sins that we either have committed ourselves or would like to commit. Having someone else to blame for them frees us, at least temporarily, from having to face either our commission, our desire, or both.

If we hold resentments against others, so that we will not have to hold resentments against ourselves, then forgiving a repentant sinner means there will be one less person standing between us and a confrontation with our own sinfulness. One way of dealing with this recognition—the way of Allen's congregation—is to make sure that the forgiveness never takes place. Then, we can continue to deceive ourselves that we have no desire to do to anyone else what this particular sinner has done to us. The better way is to give thanks to God for those who ask our forgiveness because they come to us bearing a great gift: the opportunity to own up to our sinning and to seek still others' forgiveness for it. *For as you judge others,* Jesus also said, *so you will yourselves be judged, and whatever measure you deal out to others will be dealt to you* (Matt. 7:2 REB).

Privatizing

Once, I asked a former parishioner, whom I admired, why he never went to church even though his wife and children attended faithfully. As I expected he would, he gave me a straight answer, even though he anticipated that I would not be particularly pleased with it: *Preacher, I've always believed that my religion is something between God and me. I talk things over with him a lot, but just by myself. I don't feel I have to go to church to keep on track with him.* One of the most important things this parishioner still talks over with God is how he lives his life. When he does what he knows he should do, he thanks God for the opportunity. When he does what he knows he should not do, he asks God for forgiveness. *It's all done man to man,* he told me, *with nobody else listening in.*

Even though I believe that this deeply moral and spiritual man's church would be the stronger for his more active participation in it, I also think that his highly personal faith is both authentic and effective. With regard to another former parishioner, my thinking is somewhat different. Those in the church who knew her best considered her one of the most self-centered, backbiting persons they had ever met. I found my own conversations with her a continuing frustration. They were laced with superficial admissions of things she did that she knew "hacked off" one or more of her friends, followed by self-congratulatory pronouncements that God knew all about her failings and had yet again forgiven her for them. Though this young woman "took it to the Lord in prayer" regularly, she apparently listened only for the answers that she wanted to hear from the Lord, and in the process listened to no one else at all.

As different as these two parishioners probably are in God's sight, and certainly in everyone else's, they share two convictions in common with countless numbers of believers today: (1) that because sins are individual acts, the guilt for them accrues only to the individuals who commit them; and (2) that our accountability as Christians is to God alone. Whatever effect sinful behavior may have on a community of faith is of no real importance in the context of divine forgiveness. If God has forgiven the person from whose sins others are still reeling, how can they not do the same? Taking stock of ourselves all by ourselves, confessing to God directly or in the privacy of a confessional booth, doing penance that does not at least attempt to address directly the damage particular sins cause, receiving absolution privately or at one's own hands—all contribute to undermining the integrity and mission of the Christian community as a moral guide, as an agent of accountability, and as a fellowship of forgiven sinners.

Everyone knows the major reason the problem of pedophile priests almost overwhelmed the Roman Catholic Church in this country: Widespread cover-ups put the interest of protecting church institutions ahead of serving the needs of the abused faithful. Less widely discussed is another reason, one that is of particular importance to the present discussion: naive overevaluation of the power of private confession and penance to remake individual sinners in God's image. Trusting for too long in this traditional understanding and practice, church leaders blithely accepted the promises of unscrupulous priests not to abuse again, put them under the church's protection, and unleashed them on still more unsuspecting victims. Unfortunately, although their collective sin has been fully exposed for what it is, some church leaders still seem hesitant to confront this problem in the way that a genuinely Christian community should: by bringing things out into the open, putting all of the resources of the church at the disposal of those whose first priority is to help victims heal, instituting measures designed to ensure that the offenses will not happen again, and asking forgiveness instead of offering excuses.

The notions that sin is individual only, and that accountability is only a matter for each individual to work out with his and her Maker, blind us to the power of one individual's sinning to conscript and corrupt others in the same church. Many people in Allen's congregation fell under the sway of one member's sinning, not by sinning in the way he did, but by allowing their bitterness to overwhelm their disposition to seek reconciliation through mutual understanding and forgiveness. A few Roman Catholic leaders, smugly assured that keeping their church scandal-free was what God wanted above all else, gradually seduced other colleagues to join them in a conspiracy of silence and protection of their own. The waves one person's sinning stirs up in a community of faith inevitably draws others into their wake.

Clericalism

During a conversation about the calling to ordained ministry, an Episcopal student of mine, whom I will call Dave, once shared with me his primary reason for wanting to enter the priesthood: to receive the authority to absolve people from their sins. At first, it seemed to me that Dave held an uncommonly narrow view of the priestly office. As we talked further, I began to understand better why the priest's role as confessor was of particular importance to him. *I've never been able to deal very well with my own guilt*, he said, *unless I can talk about my sins to someone authorized to hear my confession, to help me work out the appropriate penance, and to give me absolution in the name of Christ.*

In the interest of furthering the dialogue, I shared with Dave my own view that all who earnestly strive to serve Christ faithfully, and not just the clergy, are authorized by God to offer people, willing to receive it, forgiveness and reconciliation in Christ's name. Laypeople can be priests or soul friends to one another, listening caringly to one another's confessions and the struggles that lay behind them and saying to one another, "In the name of Jesus Christ, you are forgiven." Dave's reply to my "priesthood of all believers" position was interesting, insightful, and deeply felt:

> *Whether they go to a therapist or a priest, I think people are hoping to meet someone who can be for them some kind of transcendent source of power and grace. Or at least someone who can mediate the presence of such a source. For me, it's a hoping to meet Jesus and to experience his love all over again.*

Dave went on to say that, for him, it is the authority conveyed by the church to absolve people from their sins that makes priests the truly representative figures they are. Ordination is the primary source of a priest's power to communicate, on behalf of Christ and the church, God's forgiveness not only by their hearing confessions, but also in everything else that they do as priests.

From his position now as a highly respected priest and leader in his church, Dave continues to chide me good humoredly for being so indiscriminate in my way of handling sin in the church. *If everybody is a confessor,* he said once, *then nobody can really feel forgiven.* My reply, somewhat but not completely tongue in cheek, was: *If you guys are the only confessors around, isn't Jesus leaving himself a little shorthanded?* Below the surface of our theological joshing, Dave and I have always known that there are real and important issues between us, both of how we deal with individual sins and guilt in the church and of how we deal with the collective guilt of the church itself. With regard to the latter, and the topic of this chapter, the issue has become an especially serious one. Whom shall we trust now to bring about healing of the church's collective guilt? Only the members of the clergy, of whom too many have left us scandalized, angry, and dispirited? Surely the laity must play the central role in the restoration of the church to itself.

If Allen's style of pastoral leadership is any indication, it will take more than just a reenergized clergy for a church to overcome the effects of wrongdoing against its members. On the matter of pedophile priests, almost everyone now agrees that there is little likelihood of lasting change on the part of American Catholic leaders until the laity becomes genuinely empowered to contribute to the process. Major structural changes in Roman Catholic governance will be necessary for anything like this to occur. Presently, the church's hierarchical structure all but disenfranchises laity when it comes to assessing pastoral performance and leadership. No matter what lay review boards may say and do about their bishops' actions toward pedophile priests, the bishops will be finally accountable only to the Vatican (unless the American judicial system continues to weigh in heavily on the issue). In many Protestant denominations, my own included, the situation is not much better. Clergy take care of their own, and laypeople are all too often asked to suffer the ineptitude and even immorality of pastors with unprotesting, forgiving hearts.

My former student and now very able pastoral leader, Dave, is right to cherish the fact that many repentant Christians see in their priests' faces the loving and forgiving face of Christ. I believe that even more see our Lord's face in the faces of lay caregivers as well. Because they do, they often express to their caregivers words like these: *I can tell you things I've never told anybody—not to my family or to my friends and not even to my pastor.* Are caregivers like these not the very people the church most needs to help heal its collective guilt?

Reconciliation in a Litigious Society

A fourth hindrance to the process of healing the church's collective guilt is the willingness of caring Christians to substitute legal action against wrongdoers for reconciliation with them. With rare exceptions, litigating claims for damages is inimical to overcoming enmity between people. To illustrate, in the interest of reconciliation, alienated people are encouraged to be open with each other, to admit whatever contribution each may have made to the situation, to accept personal responsibility for harm caused, to make amends, and to allow forgiveness to do its divinely appointed work of restoring the broken relationship. By contrast, in the interest of litigation, disputants are encouraged to avoid personal contact with each other except in the company of lawyers, to multiply their accusations against each other, to disclaim responsibility, to resolve conflict by determining blame and receiving compensation, and then, wherever possible, to erect a permanent wall of alienated silence between all parties to the actions settled. Is it any wonder that the early church strongly discouraged brothers and sisters in Christ to take one another to court at all?

Since the subject of this chapter is the healing of collective guilt, the effect of utilizing the judicial system to rectify things between individuals is an issue whose importance can only be noted in passing here, without further elaboration. The primary concern of the present discussion is the effect that the current litigious climate in our country can have on the church's assumption of responsibility for its collective sins and guilt. By "the church" here is meant the church that has been central to the vision of Protestantism from the sixteenth century to the present: the church always reforming itself in the image of Christ (or: *ecclesia reformata sed semper reformanda*). For the truly reformed and reforming church to be an effective witness to God's great work of forgiveness and reconciliation in the world, it must embody that spirit in its own life, by confessing its own wrongdoing openly, by seeking the forgiveness of those it wrongs, and by inspiring all of God's creatures everywhere to become more forgiving in their own lives. There can be no place for dissembling about collective guilt, whatever the cost may be of resisting the temptation to engage in it.

To be sure, the church has both the right and responsibility to defend itself and its members against excessive, false, and fraudulent claims upon its resources. And its members have the right and responsibility to insist that what they give to the church for the purposes of honoring God and serving God's people in the world be used for just these purposes, not to settle unjustifiable claims prematurely for reasons of expediency. However, even in the face of legal actions that portend catastrophic consequences for the church, defensive strategies that put church interests ahead of the well-being of those the church harms are nothing short of blasphemous. Whatever might be gained by means of such strategies—by delaying tactics, for example—comes at the expense of the church's very soul.

From the standpoint of the ministry of reconciliation, the greatest strength of our legal system is also its greatest weakness. Its aim is the determination of truth and justice in fair and impartial proceedings conducted by advocates who do everything in their power to make the best possible case for those they represent. The problem is that part of what makes one side's case attractive is putting the other side's in the worst possible light. That both sides of a particular dispute might have merit is a possibility rarely entertained. In most proceedings, the rule of thumb is that one side must prosper at the expense of the other. Our legal system rewards worthy adversaries more than it does committed peacemakers.

Just as the church is justified in depending on our legal system to protect its rights, its members are justified in looking to this same system for help when their church acts wrongfully against them. Lawsuits threatened, damages awarded, and jail time imposed may make healing possible for at least some of those wronged. Compensation for their suffering is justified, and the courts may be the only way to gain it when their churches and church institutions fail to address their concerns honestly.

Not everyone who follows this course will be successful, though, and they will need and deserve other kinds of support if they are to find peace for themselves. Will the church be up to the task? Will church leaders merely leave the offenders to savor vindication and pretend that nothing needs to change? Or will they take up the cause of the victimized and keep pressure on their exonerated brothers and sisters to come to terms with their self-righteous denials? Will they see to it that those who have not received justice from the courts receive nurture from other quarters of the church? For those whom the legal system fails, the very credibility of Christ's ministry in the world may depend upon how well the church lives out the right answers to these questions.

And what of those who prevail in their legal actions against the church? Will they receive the help they need to find their way back into the redemptive and equipping fellowship that is the true church of Jesus Christ? Having exposed the worst about their own churches, will those wronged be able to forgive the people in those churches who made the exposure necessary? Who will help them try? Even more important, will the churches they have successfully opposed be willing to forgive and seek reconciliation with them?

The purpose of posing the questions is not to suggest that the circumstances provoking them are ever remedied easily. Rather, it is to convey two important reminders. The first is that no matter how many wounds the process of litigation may inflict on particular church communities and institutions, the wounds of most who initiate the process are worse. Second, there is a better way of looking at wrongdoing and guilt than in terms of who is at fault and how much they can be made to pay. Seeing to it that people are adequately compensated for injuries done them by the church is important to healing the church's collective guilt, but not as important as reconciling the Christian community with those its members and leaders wrong. Not even cripplingly expensive legal judgments against it should ever get in the way of the church's continuing struggle to heal human brokenness by first healing itself.

Summary

Together, the previous chapters of this book offer a Christian understanding of human existence in the world, whose focus is on forgiven sinners sharing God's love in a spirit of forgiveness and peace. In different ways, each chapter emphasizes the importance to God's great work of reconciliation in the world of acknowledging wrongdoing honestly, along with the guilt and guilt feelings that accompany it. There can be no genuine reconciliation with those we wrong, and with those who wrong us, without facing the consequences of the wrongdoing itself and what we must do together to overcome them.

Accepting responsibility both for wrongdoing and for achieving reconciliation on the far side of it is never easy. On the one hand, the very act of bringing wrongdoing into the open can and often does arouse a spirit of judgmentalism too intense for love to dissipate. On the other, the more tedious that acrimony between people becomes, the more tempted they may be to settle for peace at the price of glossing over real guilt entirely. How to steer a course between these two extremes has been the major practical concern of the book.

To the previous discussions of reconciliation in individual relationships, this final chapter has added an exploration of reconciliation between individuals and their churches, and of the indispensable role that effective pastoral leadership plays in bringing it about. Expressed in familiar, time-honored language, one of the most important responsibilities of pastors as shepherds is to protect their flocks from predators both outside and inside the sheepfolds. For fulfilling one part of this awesome responsibility, pastors in our country receive a great deal of help from the American system of government itself; the commitment to protect religious freedom for all goes a long way toward ensuring our churches' freedom from outside constraints and threats. For fulfilling the responsibility to protect the church against wrongdoers inside its own sheepfold, however, our shepherds must rely on something else: God's ongoing guidance; their own attunement to it; and an active and involved laity willing and equipped to shepherd the flocks with them. With God's help, pastors and laypersons together will be able to deal with predators in their midst, not merely by removing them from the sheepfold, but by helping them become better Christians and, then, effective shepherds themselves.